19 —
43145
R

The Now and Future Church

THE NOW AND FUTURE CHURCH

The Psychology of Being an American Catholic

EUGENE KENNEDY

Doubleday & Company, Inc.
Garden City, New York   1984

A version of the chapters "The Popes in Transition" and "The Now
and Future Church" first appeared in *Notre Dame Magazine*.

The chapters "Called Out of Bondage: Joseph Campbell on the
Religious Consciousness of the Space Age" and "Theologian for the
Now and Future Church—Karl Rahner," copyright © 1978/79/80/
81 by The New York Times Company. Reprinted by permission.

Library of Congress Cataloging in Publication Data

Kennedy, Eugene C.
    The now and future church.

    Includes index.
    1. Catholic Church—United States—History—20th century.   2. United
States—Church history—20th century.   I. Title.
BX1406.2.K444   1984   282'.73
ISBN 0-385-19040-9
Library of Congress Catalog Card Number 83-20574

For Sara
and
For These Great People of the Church
Mary Louise Schniedwind
Dan Kane
Frank J. Kobler

CONTENTS

INTRODUCTION

This book is a series of reflections on the changes of consciousness that have taken place within the American Roman Catholic Church during the twentieth century. Its purpose is, therefore, psychological, to deepen our understanding of an intensely personal and communitarian experience.

The century took its shape, as a tree from a twig, from the first decade of what seemed the advent of modern times. The extraordinary events of those years left an imprint on the American Church which can still be felt in the lives of millions of Catholics who have seen their Church seem to change dramatically in the last generation. This is a personal story and is, therefore, told in terms of the personalities—popes, priests, and scholars—who reflected the trends of their age. It is a tale with which every adult Catholic who can remember at least as far back as John F. Kennedy's election will be able in some measure to identify. Younger Catholics will find the space age and the changes in religious symbolism which it has generated more comfortable and familiar territory.

The first few years of this almost concluded century witnessed the gathering of people and events whose impact on Catholic life and its present direction has been staggering. It was not only the period in which men learned to fly and Pope Pius X succeeded Leo XIII on the throne of Peter, but it was a time of theological excitement hardly matched since in the American Church. Around the turn of the century, the man who would become Paul VI was born, as were two scholars whose genius at penetrating the core of mythology and theology is beyond comparison in the century as a whole, Joseph Campbell and Karl Rahner. The seeds of the century were all sown at its beginning. That is an essential insight in tracing the changes in Catholic awareness that have unfolded across the remarkable decades since.

EUGENE KENNEDY

The Now and Future Church

PATTERNS

An Overview—
The End of the Immigrant Church

ARCHBISHOP John Patrick Cody arrived in Chicago on a sultry August day in 1965. The fireman's son who had achieved his lifelong ambition to head the country's largest diocese was already as out of date as the Panama Limited passenger train on which he arrived. Nothing really ever went the way that Cody wanted it in the great diocese that sat like a royal crest above the spreading continent. The late Cardinal Cody will be remembered not so much for the last months of his life when, frail and Rooseveltian, he waited for death to deliver him from federal investigation, as for the symbolic meaning of his passing. Buried with him was something that was over when he came to Chicago: the immigrant phase of the American Catholic experience. Chicago's new archbishop, Joseph Cardinal Bernardin, following the themes of his mentor, John Cardinal Dearden, represents the new style of leadership of postimmigrant Catholicism. The placement, early in 1984, of new archbishops in

Boston and New York and the prospect of fresh appointments in Philadelphia and Los Angeles within another year, strongly confirm this interpretation. Postimmigrant Catholicism has come of age with a cohort of bishops—collegial, moderately progressive, utterly orthodox, reflecting a balance of tradition—strongly shaped by the Dearden-Bernardin spirit.

The Catholic immigrant experience can be divided into two great eras, the first of which, stretching across the last century, saw the Church grow comfortable with American ways. Under extraordinary leaders such as Bishop John England of Charleston, South Carolina, Archbishop John Ireland of Minneapolis-St. Paul, and James Cardinal Gibbons of Baltimore, the Church was happily open to democratic ways. As the twentieth century dawned it verged on a theological and intellectual renaissance that held great promise for the future of American Catholicism. The second epoch of the immigrant Church followed the repression of this brief but extraordinary period of scholarship and enthusiasm after Pope Pius X condemned the alleged heresy of Modernism. There followed the solemn procession of autocratic princes of American Catholicism who oversaw a period in which the dust of the energetic building of the physical plant of American Catholicism hardly settled: convents, schools, and churches rose everywhere.

This is the Church remembered by many adult Catholics, for it fashioned a way of life within the host Protestant culture that was tight, intellectually narrow, and wrapped in an invisible and largely impermeable membrane that resisted social osmosis with the rest of the country. It was also the most successful era of development in the history of the Roman Catholic Church. This Catholic structure defended itself proudly against doctrinal and moral compromise; it was, above all, obedient to the authority which was exercised for generations, without any serious challenge, by its bishops and clergy and other religious teachers. This immigrant Catholicism was, in fact, held together by the vigorous churchmen who retained their power over their flocks by exercising it regularly on an infinitely detailed category of behaviors, ranging from what the faithful could eat on Fridays to what they could think or do in the innermost chambers of their personal lives.

The regimented immigrant Church sank deep foundations in large cities such as Chicago, New York, and Philadelphia, which attracted the largest numbers of Catholics from other countries. They grew comfortable and powerful, almost casually, as they moved into and made their own police and fire departments along with educational systems and, of course, city halls in large urban centers. Protestant Americans may not have been anxious to share their monopoly of power with Catholics (on Reformation Sunday in the month before John Kennedy was elected some Protestants were asked to stand up and be counted against ceding their rightful White House franchise to a Catholic) but they could not, in the long run, fight off these popish loyalists who by their numbers and their energy were taking over in so many areas.

The leaders of the Catholic immigrants—indeed, the only educated persons among them—were the clergy who, standing at the center of their primary social unit, exacted obedience to the faith and served as arbiters, translators, and as supporters and defenders of their flocks as they adjusted to American ways. Huge, cathedral-like neighborhood churches stand everywhere in urban America today as reminders of the surging vitality of the immigrant era. Catholics in many cities still regularly identify themselves in terms of their parishes instead of their street addresses. "I'm from Immaculate

Heart, where are you from?" The greatest nineteenth-century intramural crisis of the American Church had foamed out of the struggle to coordinate the various national parishes under the authority of the local bishops. The parish was the stable and stabilizing center of the immigrant's existence.

One of the ironies of the present time is the overbuilt condition in which the Catholic Church now finds itself. The immigrant churches stand almost empty in many neighborhoods that have changed around them several times since they were erected. Catholic schools fulfilled their original function and can no longer be supported; vocations have dropped dramatically. This decline in the absolute number of Catholic schools and in priests and religious does not signify a weakening of faith so much as the close of the highly successful immigrant period of American Catholic culture. Catholics educated their children to broaden the possibilities of their advancement in America. They achieved that goal with the result that a well-educated, theologically sophisticated generation of Catholics came to maturity at midcentury. They no longer perceived the priesthood and religious life as dominant choices for their lives and they were well aware of the possibilities of lay leadership in a variety of Catholic causes. Few understood, however, that such progress was bound to change the balance of power in the American Catholic Church.

The Second Vatican Council was born of similar ferment within the Church in Western Europe. The council is mistakenly blamed for causing changes in the Church. It was rather an event generated by changes that had taken place earlier in the century for Western Catholicism. It was an already transformed archdiocese of Chicago which Cody—rotund, beaming, confident, with no intuition of shadowed days ahead—entered majestically as the city of his ecclesiastically ambitious dreams. Some of Cody's subsequent clashes with the laity arose from his administrative efforts to deal with the far advanced changes in Chicago's Catholic life. Making nobody happy, including himself, he spent his years closing down and auctioning off the no longer productive physical assets of the immigrant inheritance, bargaining strenuously with the lay Catholic teachers' union, and holding off the democratic demands of his priests. He fought a rearguard action against the inevitability of history, convinced that he was defending the faith. In fact he was defending, naturally enough, the prerogatives of power that the immigrant Church gave to the office of archbishop of Chicago.

It was a far cry from the days when the Catholics rallied unquestioningly around their priests, forgiving their human failings generously, supporting them in ways of life usually better than their own, and elevating them to a status of almost mythic respect and dignity in the community. Priests operated not only on the parish level but in close relationship to politicians and civic officials, to whom they were often related by blood as well as belief. They helped organize the union movement that guaranteed humane conditions of work and life for their people; they marched to secure the rights of their parishioners a century before the street demonstrations of the 1960s. That generation of clergy secured a privileged position which, until only a few years ago, was granted without hesitation in cities like Chicago or Boston to anyone wearing a Roman collar. The golden immigrant age of clerical domination of the American Roman Catholic Church witnessed the extensive building programs that translated Catholic ascendancy in soaring brick and mortar terms. No diocese surpassed Chicago in the triumphs of its building programs as its parochial system became the fourth largest of any school system, public or private, in the United States. At its center, and as the great symbol of the arrival of Catholics in mid-America, rose St. Mary of the Lake Seminary on over a thousand acres an hour's drive northwest of the city in a town that came to be named Mundelein in honor of Chicago's Archbishop.

St. Mary's was the achievement, as personal and eccentric as that of William Randolph Hearst at San Simeon, of George Cardinal Mundelein, the New York-born prelate who planned the scattering of handsome Georgian buildings as the Catholic University of the West. Mundelein was the unself-conscious inheritor of the good will of the immigrant Catholics who wanted their bishops to live in houses as big and as good as those of the mayor or the governor. Having their religious leaders live on a par—and sometimes on the same splendid boulevard—with the movers and shakers of WASP America gave the Catholic people a sense of dignity and importance. The immigrants thus enjoyed vicariously the status they gave to their priests and bishops.

Mundelein lived out the role to the hilt, not only enjoying the bishop's gingerbread mansion on the edge of Lincoln Park but building himself a brick replica of Mount Vernon in which to live on the seminary grounds at St. Mary's. Traveling to and from the city in a limousine with crimson-strutted wheels, Mundelein ruled in classically imperial style. He presided in a manner that many sons of immigrants grew to love deeply as they pursued their own careers in the Church. Mundelein was the prince, the collector of art and rare books, the architect of an enormous building program, the powerful Chicago regent of the last surviving crowned head of any significance in Europe—the Pope himself.

This pervasive fascination with the regal side of the

Roman Catholic Church must be appreciated as a significant factor in attracting and sustaining loyal and energetic generations of priests and bishops in the service of
the immigrant Church. It was the rich, creamy grain
which, in the New Testament justification, the working
oxen were allowed to eat as they ground it on their
treadmills.

Americans were entranced with monarchy as the
twentieth century began. The wealthy sought marriages
with royalty for their daughters, titles for themselves,
and constructed ways of life based on European manners
and customs. They lived in castles, sometimes trans-
ported stone by stone across the Atlantic. This secular
enthrallment with the style of European crowned heads
had its ecclesiastical counterpart in the hearts and imaginations of the priests who climbed out of the immigrant
classes to places of esteem and achievement within the
American Catholic Church. John Patrick Cody, the son
of an immigrant Irishman, was familiar as a youth with
the great churchmen, Mundelein among them, who had
succeeded so spectacularly to places of authority in the
great dioceses of the country. The Catholic Church was
the great romance of their lives, for it was a treasure
house of symbols, rites, and vestments, a unique and
fascinating pageant in which a poor boy might not only
declare himself a faithful believer but also become a
prince wearing watered red silk. The panoply of regal
Catholicism, supported by the proud and the poor of its
parishioners, was a primary source of self-esteem as well
as an invitation to the ambitious and dutiful young who
would seek a place in its ranks. The generation of cardinal archbishops who dominated the major Eastern
American cities in the first half of the century—
Mundelein in Chicago, O'Connell in Boston, Daugherty
in Philadelphia, Hayes and Spellman in New York—were

autocrats who lived and ruled in unchallenged majesty, their power complete and intact until their last breaths were taken.

John Patrick Cody pursued the path that so many other American Catholic young men did on their way to positions of great power in the Church. He blended ecclesiastical ambition with a desire to serve in a personality that was perfect for the clerical world of Roman Catholicism. Jovial, dutiful, loyal to those higher in authority, Cody was a man of his times who never understood that the cultural swell of immigrant Catholicism—with its adulation of the clergy and its highly romantic version of Catholic life—had subsided by the time he succeeded to the see of Chicago. Cody had apprenticed himself to the Roman way of things—he visited Rome over a hundred times during his life—to the power and glory of the manners, codes, and vesture of the Roman Catholic Church. *Romanità* marked those destined for places of power in the Catholic Church. No people were as loyal or generous to the Pope as Americans in the first half of the twentieth century. Millions of faded papal blessings hang in Catholic homes as small footnotes to this devotion to the Pope. The Protestant fear of a Pope in the White House was generated in part by the great reverence with which Catholics regarded him.

The years immediately after the Second World War, during which seminaries and religious houses were flooded with vocations, was the triumphant high tide of the second phase of the immigrant Church in America. But a tide's highest point is precisely that at which it turns and begins to run out swiftly. The rapid tranformations of the Catholic culture took place largely because it had succeeded so well in educating and Americanizing its members. This led inevitably to the dissolution of the tight boundaries of the Catholic culture and the subsequent rapid disintegration of many of the behaviors, practices, and allegiances that once characterized a large bloc of American Catholics. The massive investment in education guaranteed a more independent, deeper intellectual class of American Catholics who were no longer ready to accept what Church leaders taught without examining it thoughtfully. They well understood and applied the traditional Catholic teaching about the supremacy of a carefully formed individual conscience. A more intellectually and morally confident generation of Catholics entered the mainstream of American life, breaking naturally rather than rebelliously free of the obsessive-compulsive grip of the once organically whole culture. Such Catholics did not despise their immigrant forebears, but they could not—and did not—imitate them in their religious practices. There was a sharp diminution of guilt over disagreeing with certain Church positions, such as the teaching on birth control, and a progressive blurring of the differences between Catholics and other groups on a wide range of moral and political issues.

The election of John Kennedy in 1960 can be seen as the symbol of the second cycle of the immigrant Church. The natural development of a vastly changed Catholic culture may be observed in countless Catholic families. The men who fought in World War I raised children who fought in World War II, who in turn raised children who protested against the Vietnam War. From grandfather to grandson there occurred remarkable changes in outlook, occupational goals, perception of the world, and religious belief and practice. Against the familiar background of such generational changes the immigrant Catholic Church died and gave birth to a new and different Catholic culture in this country. John Cardinal Cody's ecclesiastical career began in one era, prospered in another, and, not fitting well, declined in a third. His years as archbishop of Chicago will be regarded as an interlude of unavoidable conflict, a cruel transition that was, ironically, the necessary outcome of the faith and sacrifices of the immigrant Church. Cody, in fact, was profoundly a part of the unraveling culture of immigrant Catholicism. As leaf to growing tree, so was his greening, blossoming, and finally withered career, not against nature but part of it.

Other indications that the immigrant era of American Catholicism is truly ended may be found in such events as the near collapse of Catholic publishing and the rise of a new Catholic literature. Those newspapers and magazines which have survived are either subsidized by religious orders and other sources—one successfully sought a grant from the Lilly Foundation a few years before it stopped printing—or are engaged in fund-raising campaigns to keep publishing. The reason is that the stable, cohesive culture of the immigrant Church which once supported a host of special-interest Catholic magazines no longer exists. A new, self-observant, and often critical literature about Catholicism has appeared in the general literary world. John Gregory Dunne's *True Confessions,* published in 1977, was the first novel of true quality to emerge in the postimmigrant period of the American Catholic Church. A spate of lesser books and plays, some bitter, some gently self-mocking, have since appeared. They all mine the immigrant inheritance, the wondrous, regimented and profoundly human culture of American Catholicism. No such work could or did appear during the full bloom of the immigrant period. A remarkable book like *True Confessions* would then have been considered an attack on the Church rather than a novel that delivered, among other things, a subtle understanding of their own cultural passage to Catholics. Time and distance are needed for a literature of ironic self-observation to develop. Just as children must grow up and move into lives of their own to be able to criticize their parents fairly, so Catholics had to emerge from the family-like life of the immigrant Church in order to identify, appreciate, and criticize it. Not all the literature of the postimmigrant Church has equal value. The exploration of Catholicism by the artistic imagination, however, is a clear indication that the era that inspired it is at an end.

Cardinal Cody's funeral—the burial of a cardinal archbishop rather than an individual—was the last great ecclesiastical funeral Chicago will ever see, for it was the funeral of the last archbishop who attempted to rule with such absolute power. That Cody could have been the subject of a newspaper investigation, that his own judgments on the dispersal of Church funds could have been questioned by anyone: these would have been unimaginable in the earlier era of immigrant Catholicism. When scandals occurred then—as many did—they were handled in a very different way. For good or ill, the modernization of the American Catholic Church ushered in a time in which discreet procedures, the polite silence of the press, and the embarrassed tolerance of the laity are no longer automatically or easily given even to an ecclesiastical leader. That a sitting cardinal archbishop in one of the largest Catholic cities in the country should live out his last months without having answered grand jury subpoenas and under the pressure of a continuing newspaper investigation simply would not have happened during the heady days of the immigrant Church.

That it occurred at all is a sign—clearer than the loss of vocations, the closing of schools, or the widespread public lay disagreement with certain Church teachings—that a heroic period in American Catholicism has come fully and finally to a close. Cardinal Cody held tightly to his position throughout the final difficult and tragic period of his life. He was only being true to himself, his ecclesiastical education, and the world in which he had been born and raised. He believed in his own absolute authority; he died believing he had preserved it. For few men have the times ever been more truly out of joint than for John Cody. His ironic destiny was to live out his last months as a recluse, invalid and prisoner in the drafty old residence that was once the symbol of the unquestioned power of the man who was archbishop of Chicago. He lived through one last fierce dark winter and took his final breath on the night the clocks were to be turned back to salute the advancing spring.

One might argue that the terrible problems Cardinal Cody had were actually the resolution of the problem that had slowly grown during the generations in which the archbishopric of Chicago became the great ecclesiastical prize for ambitious American clerics. It was regarded as the premier position in the American hierarchy, the rich reward that went, along with its power, priests, and people, to the most loyal and, therefore, most deserving bishop in the country. The office grew to problematic size when the archbishop was made a corporation sole under Illinois law so that his authority was absolute in a secular as well as an ecclesiastical sense. By clinging to the ideas of authority that he was trained to revere, Cody unwittingly reduced the range and impact of that authority. What Cody thought he was preserving of archiepiscopal power by insisting on it even when it no longer worked very well he actually splintered into irretrievable pieces.

Cody was not, however, the only figure whose life and career became inextricably linked with the changing American Catholic culture. One should expect that Chicago, which was among the leading dioceses of the country in making progress in the shimmering high noon of immigrant culture, would also reflect the transformation earlier and more dramatically than other Catholic centers. Cody interacted with a group of priests who had been living in and enjoying the acclaim and support of the last days—like the final weeks of the sweetest of memory's summers—of that era of tribal establishment. These priests were trained in the great halls and magnificent distances of Mundelein's estate-like seminary; their summers were spent at villas four hundred miles north on the trembling edge of Lake Michigan. They worked hard but lived well as the privileged clerical class, and they were accustomed to archbishops who, if they ruled like autocrats, left them in many ways alone. Cardinals Samuel Stritch and Albert Meyer, for example, are remembered in Chicago almost sentimentally as benevolent presences even though each exercised authority that was never questioned the way Cody's was. They fit, one might say, into their age much more comfortably and were accepted, as most other cardinal archbishops were, as occupying positions in the topmost pane of the stained glass window of Catholic cultural life. In those days Catholics liked their archbishops to have unquestioned authority; that was part of the way things held together, the way things worked; God was in His heaven and all was well with the world.

This dynamic—of the archbishop as the central giver and withholder of every good gift and permission—was precisely the focus of the enormous reworking of relationships to authority which has been the great psychological task of church and state in this century. The priests who, within a year of Cody's arrival, organized a union-like Association, were, it is true, demanding more democracy within the Church. They were, however, demanding it from their father figure, the archbishop, because it was the only way that it could be granted to them within the Church's closed system. By betting everything on having a better relationship with Cody—something they never achieved—these priests accented anew the dominant role of the archbishop.

The priests of Chicago became obsessively preoccupied with their new archbishop. Cody—and his hold on power—became the subject of greatest concern for both conservative and liberal priests and people. As long as the office of the archbishop was perceived as the font and source of approbation and permission, those who seemed like rebels were, in a way they never suspected, reinforcing the patriarchal lines of the dissolving clerical Church. Lay people, as they became more confident of their own theological judgments, withdrew in increasing numbers from the white-hot edge of combat. They found that they did not need their archbishop's permission to do good, they did not need his approval in order to attain self-esteem, and they did not need the tension that the battle with the autocratic Church introduced into their lives. The sharp decline in Catholics' approach to the confessional box was an external signal of their internal refusal to subject their consciences to ecclesiastical judgment. The collapse of neurotic guilt over the pervasive possibility of mortal sin in events as trivial as eating meat on Fridays or washing a pair of stockings on Sundays—these ranked with murder and grand larceny after all—was also a sign that the structure of the immigrant Church, like that of a sagging barn by the roadside, was close to collapse.

Studies have shown that many able priests and religious gradually drift to the side of their culture, finding their own ways, using their talents on their own outside the prescribed possibilities of clerical and religious life. It is no wonder that so many religious women, such as Sister Mary Mansour in Michigan in 1982, for example, have run for political office. The emergence of a well-educated, independent, self-confident woman in American churchlife offer further signs of the disintegration of the culture which was once able to keep them subservient, even as it was able to force priests to sacrifice their innate abilities and to endure long frustrating years carrying out routine tasks under the command of their bishops. Women have liberated themselves more swiftly than most men from such suffocating experiences.

Sister Mansour's passion and trial at the hands of the archbishop of Detroit, Edmund Szoka, are a cruel reprise of the sledgehammer use of episcopal authority so familiar in earlier times. Its result was disastrous for Szoka, who lives in the past as clearly as Cody did, and who diminished his authority by exercising it so anachronistically. That a distinguished woman religious should be forced out of her order in such fashion has made the Church of Detroit, so progressive under the leadership of Szoka's predecessor, John Cardinal Dearden, seem medieval in motivation and focus. This sorry episode is counterpointed by that of a woman religious who also achieved similar statewide public responsibility at the same time in Minnesota. Archbishop John Roach of Minneapolis-St. Paul, then president of the National Conference of Bishops, saw no reason to make an issue of it. That such a juxtaposition of events could take place underscores the vastly transformed quality of American Catholic life.

The well-educated Catholics who have emerged from the immigrant culture to participate in and shape the fate of pluralistic America no longer need to pay much attention to those who comport themselves as father-figure ecclesiastics. An enlightened hierarchy presiding paternalistically over the moral lives of the Catholic people is an idea whose time has already passed. It is an attempt to restructure a nervously fathering Church that no longer exists. Catholics, in vast numbers, disagree with their episcopal leaders on subjects such as birth control. It is too late to promote a romantic, reworked Church in which bishops and priests retain a position of absolute eminence in the lives of their people. They are still respected, they are still accorded a measure of symbolic honor, but few bishops or their priests play a decisive role in the formation of the contemporary conscience. The idea of a communal Church in which Catholics and their ecclesiastical leaders live and work in a kind of family style—with no mistaking who the parents are—is a relic of the great days of midcentury reform when the smell of revolution was in the air. That era, as bubbly as champagne while it lasted, is also closed. Nothing closed it more firmly than the development of supposedly democratic ecclesiastical structures, such as lay councils in parishes. That was an effort to modify but not essentially alter the authority structures basic to the glory days of immigrant Catholicism. Patches, in other words, on worn-out wineskins.

The clerical core of the Church continues to disintegrate. The current leadership of the American Church may well represent the finest achievement of the great vocational harvests of midcentury. The present National Conference of Bishops may never be surpassed in intelligence, wit, and refinement. Freed from the shadows as well as the grip of the latter immigrant phase of Catholicism, these men still remain its fairest lineal descendants. Different in vision and awareness from their predecessors, their family resemblance to them emerges in their absolute loyalty to the Holy See and to orthodox Catholic teaching. There may literally never be another generation like them because the generous supply of Catholic vocations from which they were drawn has, at the very moment of their maturity and accession to authority, approached exhaustion. These leaders of postimmigrant Catholicism will never see a restoration of vocations from the ethnic sources which produced them. They must prepare for the reality rather than the pleasant, manageable fiction of lay people with only the appearance of responsibility in the Church.

They must also understand that, as one immigrant Church disappears, another is growing in the very states which will be foremost in national influence in the next century. The Latinos in the Southwest and the Southeast are the new immigrant Catholics, the counterparts, all these long decades later, of the people who built the American Church with their small, steady sacrifices of money and sons and daughters. These immigrants are already a source of new energy for the country and, while their attitudes toward the Church may be very different from those with which Americans are familiar, they must be perceived now as essential to its future existence and identity.

The now and future Church is already in place, its success not fully certain but its general outline plain enough to see. The power and the grandeur of the immigrant Church—the great days in which poor boys could become princes and live in palaces, or on seminary grounds, as Cardinal Mundelein did, that required a hundred gardeners—all of these were buried with John Cardinal Cody in the bishops' chapel at Chicago's Mount Carmel Cemetery.

The Dearden Inheritance

JOSEPH Cardinal Bernardin is linked in style and disposition to the man most responsible for the modernization of the American Catholic Church and, therefore, for its present ideological positioning, John Cardinal Dearden, retired archbishop of Detroit. Dearden, urbane, cultured, and learned, came out of the Irish Catholic culture that flourished around Cleveland, Ohio, where he served for a time as a seminary rector. He became bishop of Pittsburgh at midcentury and was known there, as he had been at the Cleveland seminary, as "Iron John," a strict disciplinarian out of the old school.

Pope Pius XII died in October 1958 and with him Francis Cardinal Spellman's predominant influence in the elevation of bishops to important dioceses in the United States. Only the year before, clerical wags had noted Spellman's role in moving Bishop Walter P. Kellenberg to the newly created diocese of Rockville Centre on Long Island by referring to the latter as "Spellenberg." Amleto Cardinal Cicognani, long Apostolic

Delegate to the United States, assumed new power as Secretary of State under the new Pope, John XXIII, and he switched the American source of power to his old friend, Edward Hoban, the bishop of Cleveland. A new family of ecclesiastical appointments, including Clevelander John Krol to Philadelphia, soon emerged. In January 1959, the same month in which he announced that he would hold an ecumenical council, Pope John XXIII named Dearden archbishop of Detroit. These two events would have major consequences for American Catholicism.

Dearden has described how he himself grew during the years of Vatican Council II, whose reforms he wholeheartedly embraced and introduced, with broad lay participation, throughout his diocese. But Dearden learned other things in Detroit and these, combined with his personality and the collegial vision of Vatican II, gave a distinctively American imprint to the transformation of the Catholic Church in the United States. Dearden came to appreciate the art of labor negotiations in the auto industry, to value these as a distinctively American achievement, and to understand their application to the transition period into which the American Church was swiftly heading. He also gained new influence, both for his own qualities and for his relationship to what became known as the "Cleveland Connection" in Rome. In the midsixties it was clear that he was the natural leader of the American hierarchy, even though he was not yet a cardinal and despite the fact that a cohort of autocrats— Spellman in New York, McIntyre in Los Angeles, Cody in Chicago, O'Boyle in Washington—incarnated, in their declining days, the decaying authoritarianism of the immigrant Church. Dearden was chosen the first president of the National Conference of Catholic Bishops in its newly organized format in 1966, a position he would hold for five crucial years that will someday be identified as those during which the blueprints for the present shape of the Catholic Church were, in a combination of Vatican II theology, American pragmatism, and immigrant Church know-how, carefully drawn.

Dearden, as dutiful as he was when he earned the name "Iron John," eschewed the role of charismatic reformer in order to carry out what he judged, in classic American style, to be more fundamental but infinitely less interesting tasks. He was not, in other words, naive about power. The future of the American Church depended on transforming the Conference of Bishops from a loose aggregate of men who considered themselves independent colleagues into cooperators in managing a national Church. This was no small task since the traditions of the episcopal organization that emphasized their separateness were expressed in a revered immigrant Church saying, "The bishop is the boss in his own diocese." The bishops' annual meetings at the Catholic University of America in Washington were largely perfunctory and some bishops, including Thomas E. Molloy of Brooklyn, one of the nation's largest dioceses, never attended at all. These men had not become bishops in the old Church to be anything less than they were expected and aspired to be: the sole regents of power with the last word on almost every ecclesiastical transaction within their jurisdictions. Combining them into a working conference would be something like reuniting the many kingdoms of Italy. Nonetheless, this was the unromantic task to which Dearden applied himself, adroitly moving behind the scenes with the knowledge he had gained of the inner workings of the Church in order to build a solid foundation for a body of bishops whose capacity to work effectively together would determine the future of the official Church in America.

The theologian and administrator who understood labor negotiations was at work, disappointing Catholics who wanted him to be a more visible and dramatic leader while he patiently laid the foundations for a structure which he wanted to last. Patrick Cardinal O'Boyle would, for example, remain opposed to the direction the new Church was taking and fought one of the most ignoble of rearguard actions, forcing a score of Washington, D.C., priests to resign from active ministry because of their dissent over the encyclical on birth control. O'Boyle was the no-nonsense administrator to whom obedience and authority were clear-cut and central questions. Francis Cardinal McIntyre, well into his eighties, remained a vocal critic of change, leading a disgraceful attack on Bishop James Shannon, then auxiliary of Minneapolis-St. Paul, for appearing on a television program about the Catholic Church. Such men would fight to keep the power structure of the immigrant Church firmly in place; they would also attempt to deny Dearden the cardinal's hat which he received in 1969.

One of Dearden's first moves as president of the reluctantly reorganized bishops was to request that Archbishop Paul Hallinan of Atlanta release his young auxiliary bishop, Joseph L. Bernardin, to serve as the general secretary of the episcopal conference. Dearden was influential in seeing that Bernardin, a man remarkably like him in personality, intelligence, and obsessive work habits, became archbishop of Cincinnati in 1972. Thus a new family of influence in American Church polity came into being. Then forty-four, Bernardin was already highly esteemed by the other bishops, who had come to know him during his years as general secretary of their national conference. It was no surprise that he was elected their president in November 1974. O'Boyle, gruff and unconverted, left the bishops' meeting immediately afterward, saying loudly, "The only reason I came was to vote against him." It was not unlike watching an old Irish political boss ruefully regard the up-and-coming Italian who has just taken over the office of mayor, an event that had many parallels at the same time in the broader secular culture of the immigrant Church.

Far different were the comments at the Apostolic Delegation across Washington, D.C., that evening. Archbishop Jean Jadot, a French-born ally of the new builders of the American Catholic Church, held a reception for the country's bishops. "Now," Cardinal Dearden said to a friend, "Joe can move!" Step two, in other words, in strengthening the organization of the bishops and, through new appointments, gradually transforming their character and outlook to that of postimmigrant Church leaders. Bernardin was already a member of the Vatican Congregation that named bishops and a prominent figure at the international synods of bishops held regularly in Rome. He now had the position and the power to continue the restructuring of the American Church according to the practical, dialectic vision on which he had worked so intimately with Dearden for years.

Bernardin, with no peer in his capacity for painstaking, bureaucratic work—a central requirement for both successful politicians and bishops—continued to appoint a younger generation of bishops whose convictions had been formed by the events of Vatican II. No longer was a degree in canon law the essential educational preparation for the American episcopacy. That change, in itself, was to have a major impact on the American Church as the seasoning of new disciplines and new world views diluted the legalistic structuring of the Church that had been as natural as breathing to a previous generation of bishops. Still, Bernardin had his critics in the seventies, the same ones Dearden had before him. If he displeased conservatives, he disappointed the impatient progressives who wanted major changes rather than administrative readjustments in the Church. Bernardin conceived of his task as making room for the Church to develop without completely losing its shape in the process. The second half of the seventies witnessed enormous changes in Church personnel and practice, the working out, often quite painfully, of enormous cultural changes that had taken place long before.

The last of the old-fashioned churchmen, John Cardinal Cody, survived unhappily through his fiftieth ordination anniversary celebration on December 8, 1981, on the lavish grounds of the great seminary that Mundelein had built as one of the fortresslike symbols of the immigrant Church's triumph. Although most of the country's bishops attended, it was a ghost of the hearty celebrations that marked the heyday of clerical culture. The affair was made doubly poignant by Cody's conspicuously failing health and the cloud of suspicion that had trailed after him since a Chicago newspaper had begun a series of investigative reports about him three months earlier. Cody told the rector of his cathedral, the now Bishop Timothy Lyne, that it was his "last hurrah" as he prepared to celebrate and preach at midnight mass on Christmas. After that, it was in and out of hospitals, a prolonged, sad season's dying for a man who had long before been overtaken by times he never understood.

Joseph L. Bernardin, after the most intense scrutiny ever carried out by the Vatican, was appointed archbishop of Chicago in July 1982 and was named a cardinal five months after that. The circle that Dearden had begun to forge almost a generation before was complete. The postimmigrant Church, which would soon address itself to a major extramural issue, nuclear arms, would, through at least the beginning of the twenty-first century, bear the imprint of the pragmatic, collegial negotiating style that was part Vatican II, part union negotiations, part the informed gentlemen's instincts that Dearden and Bernardin shared.

This approach, which operationally recognizes the death of ecclesiastical authoritarianism, introduces a new concept of authority that realizes itself not through dictum but through methodical collegiality. That is the governing dynamic of the official Church that is meant to house and give direction to the abundant energies of postimmigrant Catholicism. Nothing could be more American than a Church deeply committed to the process of negotiation through dialogue that is the down-to-earth, sometimes maddeningly extended meaning of collegiality. The American Church faces enormous challenges from within and without over the next generation. Each of them will be dealt with through a style of discussion, revision, and compromise which will attempt to make room for as many voices as possible. The success of this strategy, which absorbs rather than sharpens conflicts between authority and obedience, will determine the success of the American Church which, through Joseph Cardinal Bernardin, is the inheritance of John Cardinal Dearden.

The Light That Failed

AMERICAN Catholics can already make out the first light mantling the palisades of the next century. They speak of a greatly changed Church, distinctively American, rich in energy and ideas, enlarged in its sense of membership, and more sure of its healthy independence from European traditions.

The century in prospect is not the twenty-first but the twentieth.

Less than a hundred years ago the American Catholic Church, as confident of its future successes as of its past accomplishments, seemed "suddenly ready," according to historian Michael V. Gannon, "to enter an intellectual renaissance, a 'golden age.'" As intoxicated with the excitement of modern times as the rest of the nation, this Church crossed the new century only to be broken within a decade on the rack of Old World authoritarianism. That swift, thorough repression of the cultural and theological ambition of American Catholicism generated the anti-intellectual clericalism that profoundly affected the Church for generations afterward.

As in the last futile wars of the European monarchs that provided the background for this drama, a generation of great promise was brutally cut down, leaving the still air, on which floated the toasts of victorious generals, filled with the stone odors of tombs. The American Catholic Church has not yet fully recovered from it. Gaze into the stereopticon for a view of the Victorian towers of New York's archdiocesan seminary, St. Joseph's, which was spread on the fold of a hill at Dunwoodie just north of the city in Westchester County. Here, in miniature, the tragedy that affected the entire American Church was acted out. The vitality of the seminary's rector, Father James Driscoll, and its extraordinary faculty symbolized the American Church's optimism about the world in which they were deeply involved. Driscoll, a native of Vermont, was, at the age of forty-three, a well-trained scholar of Semitic languages when he became president of the seminary in 1902. Grouped around him were men such as scripture scholar Father Francis E. Gigot, orientalist and biblical theologian Father Gabriel Oussain, and a progressive philosophy professor, thirty-one-year-old Father Francis Duffy, who would later gain fame as chaplain of the "Fighting 69th" in the First World War.

These men were keenly aware of the advances in scholarship which were already revolutionizing Scripture study in Europe. The Bible was not a staid collection of dead tales but a living document whose many voices could be made to speak again by those who could hear and freshly translate its languages and literary forms. The Scriptures and theology could breathe life once more and be relevant in the dawning century. Masters of scriptural languages, Driscoll and his colleagues matched the needs of the moment. Intellectual excitement still lifts off the letters of these men who represented the maturation of the first great phase of immigrant Catholicism in America. Nineteen hundred makes a rough dividing line in the history of the immigrant Church. The half century that followed seems darkly authoritarian in comparison with the nineteenth-century Church which, though filled with problems, was in comparison far more energetic, curious, and American. Dunwoodie Seminary, located along the Hudson just above the metropolitan intersection of the dioceses of New York, Brooklyn, and Newark, where already some 1.6 million Catholics lived, would, in its practices and curriculum, seem remarkably advanced even eighty years later.

Driscoll believed that the priest, instead of being trained in introspective isolation, should be educated in the heart of the world alongside the men of law, medicine, and the arts who would give shape to the new century. He worked out an agreement with Nicholas Murray Butler, president of Columbia University, which allowed Dunwoodie students to be accepted as graduate students and to attend courses at that institution at no cost. The seminarians were also encouraged to take courses when they could at New York University. Driscoll abandoned the traditional scheme of seminary lectures on topics such as "Medieval Guilds" and replaced it with a series of talks by distinguished Catholic and Protestant lecturers, including the president of Union Theological Seminary, Dr. Charles A. Briggs. Driscoll also worked out a faculty exchange program with the latter institution. One of the most poignant footnotes to the period is to be found in the 1925 action of Columbia University's Board of Trustees, suspending its arrangement with Dunwoodie for lack of use.

The already heady intellectual excitement of the semi-

nary was increased when Driscoll, responding to sugges-
tions from Father Duffy and another philosophy professor, Father John Brady, proposed to New York's
Archbishop John Farley that the faculty sponsor a professional theological journal. This magazine, which was
called the *New York Review*, proposed, in Driscoll's
words, "to discuss in a scholarly way, yet in a manner
intelligible to ordinarily cultured persons, lay or cleric,
the various questions with which the modern Christian
apologist has to deal—mainly those pertaining to Scripture and Philosophy." Archbishop Farley heartily en-
dorsed the undertaking and the first issue was published
in June 1905 with the subtitle, *A Journal of Ancient Faith
and Modern Knowledge.* As Driscoll would later write to
the editors of the Boston *Transcript,* its purpose was "not
to abandon the old in favor of the new, but rather to
interpret with becoming care and reverence the old
truths in the light of the new science. The task . . . is
not one involving doctrinal change but restatement and
readjustment—in other words, the preservation and not
the rupture of continuity."

Driscoll and his associates were, however, launching
their journal in an atmosphere charged with suspicion
about what were termed Modernist tendencies on the
part of certain prominent European scriptural scholars
and theologians. Modernism has never had a definition
as clear as its later condemnation. Rooted in European
scholarship, the controversy centered on the application
of new methods of scholarship to biblical and theological
issues. While Driscoll and his faculty proceeded to apply
their learning, especially in biblical languages and theology, to an exploration of Catholic teaching that would
reflect and speak to the religious questions of the dawning age, they were, because of their knowledge of and, in
some cases, friendship with certain Modernist scholars,

such as the English Jesuit George Tyrrell, not without their critics. Nonetheless, the fact remained that within a few short years the Dunwoodie faculty had revolutionized American seminary life and developed a learned theological journal for which there would be no parallel in the United States until the Jesuits established *Theological Studies* thirty-five years later.

The Camelot-like days of the *New York Review* were to number less than a thousand. It had begun its publication in the same year that the first articles were being commissioned for the Catholic Encyclopedia, which, although another proof of the achievement of America's immigrant Church, would also soon fall under suspicion. The blossoming intellectual life of the American Catholic Church was to be trampled by the rush of American prelates to accept the syllabus of errors, *Lamentabili,* issued by the Holy Office in the early summer of 1907. Two months later Pope Pius X's encyclical, *Pascendi Dominici Gregis,* soundly condemned a detailed listing of the errors of Modernism. The encyclical, as Gannon observes, "cautioned, *in globo,* against all systems of thought by whatever name which expounded on an evolutionary theory of religion, or suggested that the Church had reshaped external truths in every period of history according to its understanding, or otherwise threatened the validity and the stability of dogma." As a side effect, the lights were about to flicker out on one of the brightest periods of theological activity in the history of the American Church.

Although Farley offered a spirited defense of the *New York Review* against the criticisms of the then Apostolic Delegate, Archbishop Diomede Falconio, the archbishop's credibility—even his position—were imperiled through subsequent attacks on the Catholic Encyclopedia and the alleged Modernist tendencies of some young

New York priests studying in Europe. Farley reportedly emerged from an audience with the Pope that summer, his face flushed, his violet cape askew. Pius X greeted the long-delayed group of visitors who followed Farley by hurling a just-presented volume of the Catholic Encyclopedia on the floor of his library, claiming it was an evil book vitiated by suspect articles. In November the Pope, who half a century later would be canonized, issued a *motu proprio* that brought advanced Scripture study to a virtual halt by declaring binding all past and future decisions of the Pontifical Biblical Commission. The *New York Review* suspended publication the following year, claiming the lack of a sufficient number of interested readers.

The mountains were about to fall on the prophets of the American intellectual revival. Pope Pius X, in his condemnatory encyclical *Pascendi,* had cited pride as the source of doctrinal error among priests. "Pride puffs them up with that vainglory which allows them to regard themselves as the sole possessors of knowledge . . . [and] arouses in them the spirit of disobedience, and causes them to demand a compromise between authority and liberty." Such priests, he insisted to bishops, were to be employed "only in the lowest and obscurest offices." Intellectual martial law was declared throughout the Roman Church: committees of vigilance were established in every diocese to sniff out the acrid scent of heresy, teachers thought sympathetic to Modernism were to be discharged "without compunction," books and magazines, periodicals of every kind were to be censored if necessary, priests were forbidden, except in the safest circumstances, to gather in congresses.

Pius X completed the first decade of the new century by demanding that all priests take an oath against Modernism. This remained until very recent times a condition for admission to major orders and for teaching in a Catholic university. Only about forty priests worldwide refused to take the oath when it was first prescribed. Further restrictions were forthcoming that tightened the discipline of seminaries by establishing Thomism as the only acceptable mode of thought and scholasticism the only true method that could be followed. A long, dark night fell across the seminaries of America, which became rigorous, intellectually narrow training houses in which seminarians were to be kept isolated from the world and well defended against its thinking.

The new century had just begun when there arrived as bishop of Portland, Maine, the cleric who would, in himself, recapitulate, as a sturdy tree does in its thickening rings, the soul, mood, and history of the period on which the American Church had entered. William Henry O'Connell, the son of a Lowell, Massachusetts, brickmason who so despised his early tenement poverty that he later transformed it into an idyllic cottage life in a volume of manufactured letters, debarked, as if stepping out of a Henry James novel, at Portland with a retinue of Italian servants, including a coachman and a music master. He had climbed the ladder of Church authority by steering clear of Modernism and cultivating influential Roman churchmen whose style of life he embraced enthusiastically. In the fateful year 1907 he would become archbishop of Boston, a cardinal shortly thereafter, and would be distinguished for his imposition of a repressive, centralizing regime that terrified his clergy while it forced Brahmins to respect his power. "Gangplank Bill," as he came to be known because of his frequent cruises to his winter home in the Bahamas, impressed the seal of Roman authority on the second phase of the immigrant Church and tolerated no creative thinking anywhere in his archdiocese. Everything and more that Rome wanted, he autocratically ruled the Boston Church, discouraging even intellectual curiosity, and completed the second leg of the pincer attack that ended the possibility of a theological renaissance in the heavily Catholic Northeast.

Gradually the faculty at Dunwoodie was disbanded. Driscoll was the first to go, dismissed through a cablegram sent in the summer of 1909 from Rome by Farley to his vicar general. He was replaced by John P. Chidwick who, lacking any academic credentials, would be granted an honorary doctorate by Farley before the fall semester began. Chidwick's background, however, prepared him well for the task that had been entrusted to him. He had served for many years as a naval chaplain and had been cited for bravery when the *Maine* was sunk in 1898. He was a pastor who also served as chaplain of the New York Police Department. Chidwick reversed all the reforms made under Driscoll and turned the seminary into what Farley's successor, Patrick Cardinal Hayes, would proudly regard as an institutional twin to West Point. Father Francis Duffy would go into a Bronx parish and from there enter the military and achieve an ironic immortality, not as an advanced scholar, but as a chaplain hero with a statue in a square that bears his name in New York City. The brief glorious intellectual adventure of the immigrant Church, its advances still not surpassed four generations after its premature death, was, to the relief of the bishops who feared Rome's displeasure far more than an intellectually blighted clergy, at an end.

What might have happened had the light struck at Dunwoodie not been so abruptly snuffed out? Almost half a century had passed after Father Driscoll received the notification of his dismissal before there was a perceptible and hesitant stir of intellectual curiosity in the

American seminary system. It has taken a generation beyond that to bring American Catholicism to a point of openness to the world that it might otherwise have achieved generations earlier.

We cannot know, of course, what might have happened. We do know that the figures caught up in this tragedy—good men who have blurred into history—accepted their fates, that there was little if any protest at the time, and that there has been little reflection on the incident and its implications, save for the work of Gannon, since then. There have, however, been measurable effects on Catholic life, and now outriding winds, that pump up memories of the fiercest of storms, are felt again as we draw close to another century.

One of the cruelest effects of the dark night of the intellect that descended on American seminaries and religious training houses was the frustration visited on so many young men and women who gave themselves to the Church's service during those years. Their natural abilities were confined to narrow channels, to blind alleys of thought, the limits of which they strove, out of obedience, to respect and even interpret for the non-Catholic world. The price paid for never realizing their true potential, although enormous, has never been calculated. Bright, curious, and willing young men and women grew into middle age and a quiet lapse or arthritic crippling of their powers, through adjustments that were widely recognized in the Catholic culture. Indeed, they were often criticized for the very things they turned to for stimulation—for just getting through the night of an intellectually overcontrolled Church. Some had expensive or eccentric hobbies, some ate or drank too much, some just never seemed to live up to their promise. And many died before their time, worn down by the effort of conforming in an authoritarian age that did not really know what to do with them.

Perhaps the most enduring effect of the intellectual suppression all those lost and gone years ago was the new elevation and reinforcement of the clerical mentality in the American Church. Clericalism may be understood as a way of looking at the world with the priest at its center. Through it the clergyman becomes the measure of all things. It is, therefore, dangerous if the cleric is not a sensitive, broadly educated person who is comfortable with people. Many priests are not, of course, "clerical" in this fashion. Still it is a subtle infection of the spirit that many do not recognize in themselves. Clericalism, a function of the immigrant Church's idealization of the priests who presided over it from the perch of their "higher calling," is, at root, an example of authoritarianism. Under its influence the priest received deference and privilege—exceptions were to be made for "Father" —and he found it difficult to imagine a model of the Church in which he was not in complete charge. "Clericalism," the Italian statesman Gambetta once said. "There is the enemy!"

Classic clericalism has suffered reverses in recent decades—it no longer commands the awesome respect and unquestioned subsidization of its golden years—yet it remains, in friendly fire fashion, the dominant mind-set of the postimmigrant American Church. Bishop and priest still effectively control American Catholicism as masters more than stewards. They may be congenial and benevolent—there is no floridly authoritarian "Gangplank Bill" counted in their numbers—but they tightly hold the reigns on the major institutions of American Catholic life. It is natural for them; it is what they were prepared to do. It is beyond the imagination of many priests to envision members of the laity as truly capable of accepting and carrying out responsibilities of administration or ministry that are not finally under their supervision. The symptom is in the faint air of condescension, the "yes, but" . . . the "not yet" . . . and the "you must understand." It lives in the priest who, granting many freedoms and activities to his people, keeps himself at the center of things.

While bishops now turn their ears more to the Catholic community, they may do so because this is a newly defined duty rather than an earnest conviction of their hearts. The "process" of collegiality, to which American bishops, by whatever combination of routes or influences, have committed themselves, allows for endless input but as yet no decisive vote by members of the laity. At century's end, with an extraordinarily well-educated laity, there has still been no unambiguous call to their fuller identification with and responsibility for the Church.

Seventy-five years after the *New York Review* was repressed, a profound question remains: Do the bishops respect the intellectual life or do they make more room for it, liking the idea of it, but still markedly hesitant to trust its inner dynamism of inquiry? The American Catholic culture has seen the collapse or dangerous drop-off of most of the journals of reflection and opinion that flourished before and immediately after Vatican Council II. There is little evidence that the bishops or the seminary system prepare priests who either encourage or value a renaissance of Catholic intellectual activity on a broad scale. Some critics, such as Notre Dame's Richard McBrien, feel that the Catholic clergy is undergoing a generalized loss of quality and an increased passivity of character that intensifies clericalism.

As we draw closer to the year 2000 we would hardly be mistaken to suppose that the hierarchy would like to lessen rather than encourage theological research and debate, for example, on such issues as the role of women and the possibility of their ordination in the Roman rite. Maneuvers strangely reminiscent of century-old events have again been initiated to keep things under control. The Pope has, for example, established a commission that is to report to Rome on the experimentation in life-style, training, and apostolates of religious men and women in the United States. This follows a major investigation of American seminaries that was also ordered by the Pope. Only in Brazil has a similar inquiry been carried out. Rome remains uneasy about the New World. The current exploration was reportedly begun after reports had been forwarded to Rome about a sex education course that was being offered under the auspices of a Midwestern seminary. Although the series was designed for the general public, its very scheduling proved disturbing to Vatican authorities, who were almost successful in preventing one of the involved seminary educators from being raised to the episcopate. Intervention at the highest levels of the National Conference of Catholic Bishops was required to forestall this disciplinary response. The American bishops have cooperated in the investigation of seminaries so far, hoping thereby to supply a balance it might otherwise lack. It is not, one feels, anything like the events at Dunwoodie, but observers wonder if the spirit that crushed the Dunwoodie renaissance still burns brightly in Vatican windows.

There is an echo from the beginning of this century in the appointment of Archbishop John J. O'Connor to New York for he, like Father Driscoll's successor of long ago, was a Navy chaplain noted for his traditional ways. In his brief tenure as bishop of Scranton, O'Connor addressed a twenty-three-page letter to his priests in which, with military discipline obviously in mind, he told them that if they did not accept their assignments, they might end up without assignments at all. But, of course, it is now the end of the century and all very different. And yet . . .

Such attitudes brought to ruin the extraordinary developments that were set, like a light on a mountaintop, on the first rise of the present century. The great questions that were asked during that brief moment of illumination have never since been posed quite so confidently or with so much concern and loyalty to the Church. They were questions about the rich mysteries of scriptural revelation and the language in which they could best be spoken freshly and freely to the modern world. Will we this time listen for the answers?

The Inevitable Tide

On the twentieth anniversary of Vatican Council II in 1982 a predictable set of retrospectives appeared in both secular and religious periodicals assaying that gathering's effects on the life of the Church. Critics hailed or damned it, progressives pointing to a more vital, world-oriented Church that issued from it like a destined biblical child; conservatives suggested that a demon had been delivered who had ever since profoundly troubled the once confident soul of the Church. Nobody denied the turmoil or the pain that, in large or small measure, Catholics of every station experience during the generation of change that followed the council. Catholics emotionally engaged by the council continue to find it difficult to make out its shape or meaning.

Few, for example, perceive Vatican II as an event in a powerful tide of change that had already been running at the full through the Church for a century. The repressive actions which had taken place earlier in the century against theological speculation, with their concomitant effects on seminary training, religious life, and diocesan administration, retarded but could not stay the process of transformation that was already fully and irreversibly moving forward. Vatican II's document, *The Church in the Modern World*, by its very title described accurately an organism that, even when trying to look the other way, rode in time and place with every other human community. The Church has always lived in and with the world, heaving and buckling in unison with all Western institutions as they struggled to enter the modern era. Even the seminary investigation of the eighties, reminiscent of the repression of the 1900s, will not be able to stay the progressive change under way—it may delay it slightly and cause unnecessary pain—but it will not stop the clock.

The central problem of Western institutions has been and remains that of authority, the very challenge with which the Catholic Church dealt, and to some degree resolved, through the combined experience of Vatican I and Vatican II. Profoundly disordering, this has not been disastrous and has proved the Church's liveliness even when it appeared to float in self-induced suspended animation. An appreciation of the Church's bonding to history allows us to understand more positively many of the phenomena, such as the drop in priestly and religious vocations, which have been used to prove that Vatican II subverted the faith of our fathers. It would, on the other hand, be naively optimistic to claim that every transformation in church life since Vatican II has been a triumph. False starts and disappointments, especially in areas that show, such as the liturgy, have at times seemed to outstrip positive accomplishments. These reforms will one day be reformed themselves and are only incidental in the life of a Church which, far from dozing during great moments of history, has been steadily on the move. The Church may, in fact, be ahead of many other human institutions in the manner in which it has reworked its internal relationships, especially those connected with authority, and be better prepared than people expect for life in the twenty-first century.

The early-century age of monarchy had already come to an end by the time those fated look-alike cousins, the King of England, the Tsar of Russia, and the Kaiser of Germany assumed their already trembling thrones. The modern world has been engaged in a bloody struggle for generations to shake free of the oppressive hierarchical model of government. This revolution in relationships continues to this day in the Third World where, beneath the tragic bloodstained confusion, may be discerned a quest for a more equitable society that is directly descended from the revolutionary disruptions of the ragtime era. The twentieth century has been an earthquake of history during which crowned heads fell and massive countervailing experiments of socialism and democracy have been locked in combat, generating tension throughout a world that had thrown away, but sorely missed, the certainty of position and identity that was delivered by the hierarchical model of government.

One of the most salient developments of our times is the spasmlike surge for equality felt even in stable democracies such as the United States. It has challenged these governments to inspect and revise their attitudes toward minorities, the disadvantaged, and women. The contributions and dislocations flowing from the pursuit of this equality is one measure of the world's attempt to resolve the problem of authority by working out new relationships throughout society. The United States has experienced obvious and continuing difficulties, for example, in defining or dealing adequately with a concept of healthy authority. Americans mistrust leaders, professionals, elites, experts, and each other. Absorbed with themselves and their personal rights, they find it difficult to establish relationships that transcend self-interest. In short, America struggles, howsoever ineffectively, with the problem of the age: What is the role of authority in personal and public life? Despising and pulling away from authoritarianism, we have yet to refurbish the notion of authority as a fresh and essential constant in truly human growth. The progressive dehumanization of life is always a symptom of a society that does not or cannot appreciate healthy authority.

The Pope may have been the last crowned head in Europe to fall, largely because Vatican Council I had reinforced the monarchical authority of the Pope through the declaration of infallibility. That doctrine was politically useful to Pius IX, who was in constant and intimate communication with the powerful sovereigns of Western Europe. The papacy had always been deeply entangled with emperors, some of whom, like the head of the house of Hapsburg, retained until this century veto power over a conclave's choice of a Pope. The concept of infallibility, however, has been hotly debated inside the Church ever since. Theological arguments aside, the proclamation of infallibility now hangs like a dead cardinal's hat from the vaulted sanctuary of the Church, an ornament from the dead era of authoritarian government.

There is no question that the proclamation of infallibility made the Pope an immense international figure and a more powerful symbol of Church unity and authority, particularly popular in the United States. No country has ever been more loyal or generous to the Holy See than America; no faith has ever anchored itself for so long in the sureness of a right order of things ordained by God presided over by the Holy Father as head of the Church,

Christ's vicar among us. The obsessive-compulsive caste of American Catholic life which was the foundation for the enormous accomplishments of the immigrant Church depended on a vigorous hierarchical model of Catholicism with the Pope at its pinnacle. That was the structure that was already under siege at the first light of modern times.

Vatican II did not come out of thin air like a temptation or an old Pope's whim. John XXIII had lived in and through the anachronistic tumult of the Church and the world as they sought to find their way into the new order of things. The code of canon law, promulgated in 1917, the first large-scale presentation of ecclesiastical regulations for the entire Latin Church, was, because of its monarchist assumptions, out of date even as it was distributed. It flourished in the twilight of the times from which it arose. It was enormously influential in keeping the fabric of immigrant Catholicism in America intact. With intellectual inquiry stifled, it presented a faith of rules and expectations, clear directions for the good life. In short, the framework for the obsessive-compulsive style which characterized American Catholicism for generations and made possible many of its enormous achievements, including the staggering number of vocations that it produced until the last generation. It supported a Catholic community that was self-contained, dutiful, and somewhat defensive, a community that, as historian William Halsey has noted, clung to its innocence about the rational, purposive character of contemporary life long after other segments of the population, largely because of the death and horror of World War I, had lost theirs. American Catholicism retained its vigor and optimism about life while many Protestant groups, by their own account, were losing their confidence in their American mission.

American Catholics were, in a real sense, riding the high tide of the duty bound immigrant culture at the very moment that John XXIII called for an ecumenical council. In 1959 seminaries were jammed, dozens of others were on the drawing boards or in the planning stages, and, as schools, they were beginning to exhibit signs of breaking away from the rigid anti-intellectualism that had characterized them for fifty years. American seminary systems began in the 1950s, for example, to abandon the European-like divisions they had long observed between their minor and major departments and to transform them into four-year institutions after the model of American education. American seminaries sought accreditation through regional agencies rather than shaping their own standards, independent of the world around them, as they had for years. They were awakening from a long slumber, not into a golden age, but just in time to bring an end to the closed, castellated era of isolation, from which, without being aware of it, they had for years been digging a tunnel of escape through timid but steady modernization.

The transformation of the American seminary system exemplifies the manner in which institutions deep at the heart of the autocratic obsessive-compulsive Catholic culture had been responding to the currents of change that, running through the world, had necessarily been running through the Church as well. These were profound impulses to reunite with the world, to break into its intellectual life and its purposive movements, to share its destiny instead of standing in judgment separate from or over it. The American seminary system did not, as some critics allege, collapse. It outgrew its outdated mode of existing, part medieval monastery, part school, in a world in which it did not function well as either entity. The seminary system broke in a thrust of health out of the cage into which it had been placed half a century earlier.

The questions that were debated at Vatican II had been asked repeatedly in the long, hard, war-interrupted decades that preceded it. They were not always asked openly, they were, indeed, often placed tentatively by progressive thinkers who provided the intellectual basis for the council that would be called, at least in part, as a way of answering them. A careful observer in the immediate postwar years could make out the line of an invisible structure of a new Church, groaning with all creation, waiting and wanting to be born. Vatican II was a response to the revival of intellectual life that had, along with the influx of vocations, the expansion of seminaries, and Catholic education's success in producing mature conscientious lay people, boldly and confidently reasserted itself. Vatican II meant that the Church had taken a breath and begun to think again.

This is not to say that anybody, Americans least of all, expected that Vatican II would turn out to be such a moment of change. American Catholics were, by and large, content with their faith and they interpreted, for example, the mild intellectual revival in seminaries benignly. Most American Catholics were extraordinarily docile and comfortable within the invisible boundaries of their own self-reinforcing culture. The immediate postwar period represented the high point of achievement for the immigrant phase of American Catholicism.

The seminary system was, after all, booming, with large classes being ordained for dioceses and religious orders everywhere. Hundreds of bright, able men and women presented themselves as candidates for the religious life. This Catholic culture within a culture was soon to feel itself even more fully justified and approved, to feel that it had arrived at last, through the election of the first American Catholic President. There was hardly a suspicion, much less a prophecy, that the prosperity of the Catholic presence—that its success, for example, in educating its offspring—would contribute shortly to its massive transformation. The occurrence of Vatican II would be the occasion rather than the cause for recognizing a new consciousness in the Catholic community. This changed sense of itself was the result of its own success, of the triumph of a huge educational system that had taught, among other things, the primacy of conscience, the importance of thinking for oneself, the meaning of a morality deeper than rule keeping. American Catholics were establishing themselves in society, moving into the professions, leaving many aspects of their immigrant heritage behind them, not because they despised them, but because they had grown out of them. Educated American Catholics were unconsciously preparing themselves for the enormous stimulation of Vatican II. The questions which the council proposed on a wide variety of matters expressed in words doubts, inquiries, and wonders that were not new to thinking Catholics.

American Catholics were psychologically ready for the experience of Vatican II. They had been preparing for years even as the Church in Europe had through various movements and experiments. Even those phenomena repressed by the Vatican in the fifties, such as the priest-worker movement in France, were signals of a new Church waiting to be born. The monarchical framework of the Church could no longer house the energies building throughout the Catholic world. Vatican II expressed and released but did not cause them.

A New Heaven, a New Earth

THE foundation of Vatican II was more significant than the edifice of the council. The towers of John XXIII's gathering rose on a new consciousness about human beings and their relationship to the universe and to each other. Its effects, partly uprooting and partly comforting, have caused feelings of dispossession and longing to be among our most common psychological experiences. We have, in this century, been challenged to rediscover the essential unity of the human person and of the universe, to complete emotionally the Copernican revolution whose implications, in the space age, can no longer be resisted or rejected. We earthlings have lost our psychological title to the center of the universe. If that has harmed our cosmic vanity it has also caused us to reorient ourselves drastically in a vastness that cannot be arranged in any convenient order. The notion of a divided universe, which served to support hierarchical models of church and state, has collapsed along with the religious consciousness which it so powerfully influenced. Vatican II may best be understood as an aspect of the revolution in fundamental symbolism through which we have passed in the twentieth century.

Part of the pain of living through this epoch comes from taking a free fall into a universe in which we once knew our place: until now we rode the blue, gemlike earth at the center of everything. That imaginative construction allowed us to speak of a heaven and earth divided and supported a graded spiritual and psychological geography of the human person. Spirit and flesh were thus at odds as we spoke easily of higher and lower faculties, of mind and body, of natural and supernatural planes of existence. The Christian life could be neatly ordered according to this pyramidal conception of the universe. Heaven stretched above us, a blessed place to which we prayed to make passage after leaving this earth behind. Various central teachings of Catholicism depended on a multistory universe. Christ ascended into heaven and the Blessed Mother was assumed bodily into that same distant abode to be there physically with her son. This literal rendering of dogma according to heaven and earth as upper and lower tiers of existence remains familiar to most believers. How else can we think of such things, how understand them if the earth is no longer the stage around which, as for a great production, reality is arranged? The space age demands that we reimagine the religious significance of these events, that we understand them as a special language, that we reinspect the map, marked here with *Up* and there with *Down*, we have followed as our path of faith.

The dependence of the monarchical, triumphant Church on a pre-Copernican perception of the universe is obvious. Such as model justified a regal presence at the very top who could claim, as earthly princes did, a divine right to preside and rule over the lower echelons of

believers. The Pope was emphasized as this kind of hierarch as the royal trimmings of thrones, crowns, and
ranges of counts, knights, and even monsignors attest.
The declaration of infallibility heavily underscored the
absolute authority of the Pope, anchoring the entire
Christian life in an hierarchical conception of the
Church that was reflected in its language, attitudes, and
religious practices. Everyday Catholicism in the immigrant American Church emphasized the descending,
delegated authority of Christendom, as well as the
sharply graded notion of the good or holy life.

The most perfect life was that furthest removed from
anything earthly; this was the life of the religious vows,
through which a person, feeling called to this state, sur-
rendered any claims to possessions, family, or the expression of his or her own will. The most perfect life was as
pure and remote from earth as a mountain kingdom.
Those who discerned this as their calling had, in a hundred symbolic ways, to separate themselves from the
ordinary world and, in most cases, become priests or
religious. Below these on the darkling plain of everyday
existence—on the lowest level of the hierarchical
Church—dwelt lay people who were thought fortunate
to have any place in the kingdom at all. The hierarchical
Church rose off their backs.

The spiritual life followed the same grand staircase
toward the upper reaches of perfection. Heaven was up
there, the earth was down here, and the Christian spiritual imagination manufactured a hundred routes,
through battles, ascents, and other muscular approaches,
by which passage might successfully be made from one
to the other. The earth was corrupt, as was the flesh. The
mind, the spirit: these were detainees in earthly forms
that generated sin and shame. The whole purpose of life
was to know and to serve God, who lived at a far remove

from men and women. The earth, its knowledge and its progress, were of little account for those who kept their eyes on the goal of this heavenly Jerusalem. So profound was the impact of this divided consciousness in the lives of Christians that it came to be summed up in a familiar phrase: Catholics could endure the world, could survive anything successfully, by offering it *up*.

Canon law provided a pattern of infinitely detailed laws as the marching orders of a monarchical Church in which authority at every level was carefully invested with power handed down from above. The entire regimen of seminary and religious life was built with an anti-intellectual emphasis on obedience to one's superiors who, as even the most revered spiritual teachers claimed, had a clear knowledge of God's will for their subjects. Those in authority, in effect, could never make a mistake. Manuals of the spiritual life literally reinforced this notion, rendering subjects almost totally passive.

This unwieldy structure could only survive if humanity held onto a divided view of the cosmos; it made sense as long as we felt, psychologically and spiritually, that the earth was a platform around which the universe displayed itself, and that God surveyed it all from a heaven that existed somewhere beyond the clouded roof of time. That conception weakened and collapsed in this century, not because of pernicious heretics who infiltrated Vatican II, not because of some modernist, religion-rejecting trend of the world, but because the human race was entering a new era in which reality could no longer be symbolized in terms of monarchy. Our entrance into the space age made these notions insupportable and unsatisfactory. The wrenching human experience of the century has a hundred different manifestations from the search for the Equal Rights Amendment to the sexual revolution. These events, no matter how untidy they may seem, are signals of a massive effort to find ourselves, to sense our human unity and our inter-personal equality, to experience ourselves anew now that the great gash across the skies and across ourselves has begun to heal.

We can see ourselves better now because of space exploration—the world in the heavens rather than divided against them—but we are having enormous difficulty assimilating this reshuffled order of existence in which there is no up or down, no hierarchical pattern to rationalize the styles of imperial life that had begun breaking apart under the weight of the future in the last century.

The terrible suppression of intellectual activity in American seminaries at the beginning of the century was the Church's baffled, authoritarian reaction to the changes in consciousness that were already well under way. The learned rector of Dunwoodie, Father Driscoll, sensed that a new understanding had to be fashioned for the languages of the Scripture; he appreciated the need for priests to read these and the theology built on them accurately and to live comfortably in and with the world as it set out on the great intellectual and scientific adventures of the twentieth century. His abrupt replacement and the suppression of the *New York Review* stand as the sorriest symbols of the enormous weakness that lay curled within the strength of the immigrant Church: its power to command military obedience.

The immigrant Church functioned very well, leaving an enormous and distinctive cultural imprint on its members, precisely because it adhered to and embodied the monarchical model so thoroughly, mistakenly identifying it with gospel essentials. The major psychological characteristic of the immigrant Church was its pervasive obsessive-compulsive atmosphere, an ideal environment for its obedient achievements. An understanding of how profoundly this dutiful style permeated Catholic life enables us to interpret the changes of the last generation more accurately and with less alarm. The emotional life of the immigrant Church was closed, highly regimented, carefully reinforced with rewards, and dependent, in the final analysis, on a strong central authority for its operational success.

Obsessiveness is a psychological style through which a sense of approval and well-being is achieved by pleasing authority in two ways: through conscientiously carrying out its wishes and by avoiding those actions which might incur its displeasure. The engine of the immigrant Church depended on this rich mixture of fuel. This is not to deny or to minimize the significance of the gospel or of the basic teachings of the Church as the fundamental motivation in the lives of the immigrant believers. It is to observe, however, that the structure of the Church in which they professed their faith was ideally suited to the management of approval and the assessment of guilt that are the essential dynamics of the obsessive-compulsive style. This was implemented through authoritative postures which demanded obedience to Church doctrine and practice in a minutely detailed manner on matters that affected almost every phase of a believer's life. To please God was to keep these regulations; to avoid the guilt of displeasing Him was to avoid even the thoughts or occasions of possibly failing to keep the regulations. This led to a highly distorted sense of values about the relative gravity of the events of the Christian life.

The structure could not have generated so much dependent behavior had there been less emphasis on the primacy and power of authority. The Church had the operational influence to command obedience, not only through the threat of eternal punishments, but also

through a variety of socially controlling temporal punishments. So powerful was the social identification of
immigrant Catholics with the acceptable doctrines and
disciplines of the Church that families would shun members who departed, through marriage to a non-Catholic,
for example, from the rigid expectations on their behavior. Excommunication was a doomsday weapon in the
immigrant Church, for it cut a person off from his or her
roots, family, and community. These realities have been
celebrated often enough in the sometimes bitter
memoirs of the last twenty years. No one can doubt,
however, that, because of the cohesiveness of the immigrant Church that flowed from its commitment to
Church authority, it successfully created its own communities within the broader American culture, punished
effectively those who deviated from its norms, and mar-
shaled enormous, single-minded strength for the
achievement of ecclesiastical and political goals. Its obsessiveness was an awesome source of strength.

Tied to this submissive environment was, among other
things, the vocational supply of seminarians and candidates for the religious life. Vocations were presented,
with theological accuracy one might now question, as
invitations that could not be turned down even by those
reluctant to accept them. Within the immigrant culture
a vocation was a blessing on a family as well as a source of
social esteem and privilege. The dutiful acceptance of a
"felt" calling, the submission of the self to Church authorities, the rejection of the world and its standards:
these were powerful dynamics in attracting extremely
talented sons and daughters to the service of the immigrant Church. The vocational supply of this Church was
dependent on an obsessive-compulsive social structure
that was held in place, as long as it lasted, by authority
that often expressed itself as authoritarianism. This was

essentially a hierarchical culture which, at its zenith in the first part of the century, accomplished more, perhaps, than any comparable group in the entire history of the Church. With typical American verve and energy it built a physical Church without parallel, an educational system of extraordinary effectiveness, while glorying in the obedience it gave lavishly to its authority figures. Not even its most gifted members, aside from its estranged writers and poets, had the distance to observe with any saving irony the tightness of the Church's grip on its members' lives.

A splendid aura of innocence rose from the highly disciplined, achieving immigrant Church. This immense and generous effort was cabled in place by the authority which decisively rewarded and punished its members. The field of vocations well illustrates the core of its obsessive-compulsive dynamic. The psychological sense of obligation to accept a vocation was paralleled by a fear of guilt if one should question it or withdraw without approval from a training program. The superiors would make all such decisions and those who did leave on their own were asked to do so discreetly, breaking off all social contact with their former friends after they reentered the world. They were made to feel that, in some essential way, they had failed; they did not have the "stuff" to persevere, they would always be second best after that. This closed self-reinforcing pattern idealized the acceptance of authority's wishes and subtly but unmistakably disapproved of any contrary intention or action.

The success of the immigrant Church may have rested on the fact that basically healthy men and women were able to survive their training and not let it permanently affect the soundness of their common sense. Still, the gradient of approval/disapproval was central in deploying and maintaining the thousands of priests and religious who entrusted their lives to the judgment and decisions of Church authority. That was an inheritance of the hierarchical model of the knowable world. Authority was not to be questioned and we were to know and keep our places in the grand providential scheme of things. As the servants lived downstairs, perceiving themselves as blessed by their destiny to serve great families, so the laity and the average priest and religious were to find contentment in accepting their roles at the bottom levels in the great structure of the Church.

Such a world looks charming and secure in retrospect, especially when we filter out the frustration and suffering among priests and religious that were abundantly present if unacknowledged at the time. That incarnation of the Church was dependent on things remaining stable, on the sociological conditions of Catholicism being frozen so that the turbine of unquestioned conscientiousness could continue to hum. That wonderful, triumphant remembered immigrant Church was, however, undoing itself through the very enterprises that its massed and concentrated energies made possible. It was educating itself, changing the vocational possibilities and goals of its children, transforming itself from within at the very time that a new consciousness about human experience was reworking its assumptions from without. Its very achievement—that it worked so well—doomed it. It could not teach its sons and daughters to think for themselves and expect that this would not change them into more independent, less authority-ridden Catholics. The immigrant Church could not sustain its integrity as a closed hierarchical system as played-out monarchies collapsed all around it. The immigrant Church could not hold itself together as a divided and graded social entity as the world began to grasp that such a model did not reflect the far deeper mystery of the unity of the universe and the related unity of the human person.

The great symptom and sign of the collapse of the excessively dutiful psychology was the evaporation of guilt in the ordinary experience of millions of Catholics. They could no longer be rewarded or punished in terms of insinuated or rumored guilt. Vatican II validated an intuition that had been growing close to consciousness in the Catholic community for many years. Lacking the authoritarian capacity to dictate the parameters of guilt, the immigrant Church witnessed a loosening in all the structures that flowed from its obsessive-compulsive ethic of authority and obedience. The vocational supply depended on that culture's remaining intact, the very thing that the constructive energies of the immigrant Church were battering apart. The decline in vocational supply can, therefore, be understood as a natural concomitant of a Church that had lost its monarchical imperialism and could no longer command unquestioning obedience.

Various interpretations have been given to the drop in vocations and to other phenomena, such as the large-scale abandonment of regular confession: to some these were proof of the secular trends of the age, the selfishness of youth, the licentiousness of twentieth-century Catholics, who had become no better than their neighbors. These are tortured explanations, however, made by people who do not understand the fundamental transformations in Catholic life and human sensibility that have occurred in the twentieth century. The Church would have more cause for concern had it remained unmoved and impervious to the dynamics of history, had it been successful in maintaining its inner life in America by insisting on an authority-obedience framework.

Predictably, many of the early debates in the era of renewal concerned themselves with authority and obedience, for it was novel, not to say revolutionary, for Catholics to raise such questions. The biblical and theological grounds for Church authority were explored even as the bishops of Vatican II drastically changed the balance of authority within the larger Church. The council restored to the bishops authority that was theirs independent of that of the Pope; the vision of a collegial, cooperative, rather than autocratic Church was being worked out. The practical outcome of the council and the era of renewal was a new structure for the exercise of authority in the Church, one that matched the enormous transformations of the century and insured that America's immigrant Catholicism—and its extraordinary social reality and achievements—had come finally to an end.

The Church,
Conscious and Unconscious

HISTORY provides abundant evidence that contradicts the notion that the Church lives essentially in and through its administrative structures. The institutional Church is far more than an institution. The Catholic Church has a vast unconscious life, a profoundly sensitive dimension through which it catches the mood of history and prepares itself to deal with it. The energies of its unconscious exert pressure on its rational superstructure, causing it ultimately to accommodate itself, often with apparent reluctance, to changing times. The Church's administration strives constantly to harmonize its various transformations so that they seem to flow in a straight, finely anticipated line of progress rather than sliding on the jagged, electrocardiogram strokes of its actual passage through history. The rational, obsessive, surface style of the Church remains in constant tension with its rich, symbol-laden, nonrational depths. That is why, after epic breakthroughs of the unconscious, as during the period of Reformation or after various ecumenical councils, there is a massive, executive effort to reestablish detailed rational control over the everyday life of the Church. But the saving historical thrust of the Church radiates from its dynamic unconscious, through which it senses and symbolizes the roiling pageant of human experience.

A rational ordering of Church life is, of course, essential to its institutional survival. That pragmatic common sense, so characteristic of administrators, explains the Church's conservative drag, as though it trailed a great anchor across the bumpy bottom of time. The Church's poetic statements, therefore, sometimes emerge in garbled form, in ways that are not at all understood by the kind of obsessive-compulsive nonpoetic person who ordinarily becomes a high Church official. The miracle is that the poetry of truth, even when filtered by them, gets through at all. Perhaps no occasion more clearly demonstrated the manner in which the Church speaks nonrationally and symbolically to its age than the solemn proclamation of the dogma of the Assumption precisely at the middle of the twentieth century. This essentially symbolic rather than devotional statement was uttered at the height of the tight autocratic reign of Pope Pius XII in the same year in which, in *Humani Generis,* he warned of the dangers of certain nonliteral interpretations of Scripture, especially of the Book of Genesis.

The declaration of the Assumption enables us to understand the manner in which the Church's unconscious processes history, grasping and reflecting its deepest surges at a level remote from the intellectual discussions which led to the proclamation of the dogma. The Church was, in fact, preparing itself and the world for the enormous reality of the new era of space, the interstellar age that was soon to replace the intercontinental frame of reference. While Church officials may have been con-

vinced that they were reinforcing a literal dogma in a
highly rational manner, the Church, more wisely than
they knew, was addressing a great poem to the world.

This poem, cloaked in the deepest symbols of dogmatic pronouncement, concerned the destiny of the
race, the direction of history, and the transforming human awareness of the century: that men and women had
broken free of the planet and its self-centered view of
the universe, that they were entering the space age that
would drastically reorder their understanding of the cosmos and of themselves. It took a non-Catholic reader of
symbols—for Catholics, obsessively distracted with the
nuances and shades of literal dogma, could hardly do so
for themselves—to identify the shimmering irony that
was the key to the meaning of the dogmatic declaration.
The literal face of the dogma—that the Blessed Mother
was physically assumed from this earth up into heaven—
was a pre-Copernican rendering of a religious event that
placed it in a geographical model of the universe that no
longer had meaning. The Assumption, thus perceived,
strained the critical faculties of educated people everywhere. It was a ghost of the majesty of its true and timely
significance.

Carl Gustav Jung, the distinguished psychiatrist, read
the larger, symbolic meaning of the Church's declaration as the most significant religious event of the century. The Assumption was the symbol of Mother Earth
returning to the heavens, of the universe's reexperience
of its unity in the age of space exploration, of the great
transformation humankind would experience in the century. Within a generation men would stand on the moon
and look back as surrogate viewers for all people to complete psychologically the great effort to see things truly
that had begun with Copernicus. The blue-green earth
was indeed in the heavens, rather than on a separate

plane from them, and we are still working out the implications of the changed realization of ourselves that flows
from this enormous and necessary journey into the stars.
The space age, far from plunging human beings into an
alien void, actually makes it possible for them to heal the
long estrangement generated by a divided model of the
universe.

The rational, administrative side of the Church stabi-
lizes such flights through the ballast of its bureaucracy
but does not read, much less compose, poetry. On the
other hand, poets would be impossible managers; their
gift is inertial guidance for the great exploratory journeys of the human race. They sense where we are, and
where we are going. Indeed, every civilization depends
finally on its poets, on those who understand the language of symbols, in order to find its way forward. The
official Church's record with poets has never inspired
confidence in its appreciation of them. The immigrant
Church of the twentieth century, which prided itself on
a unity and sense of purpose doubly bound to Roman
authority, was particularly hard on poets and writers—
on Catholics like F. Scott Fitzgerald and Eugene O'Neill
and converts like Ernest Hemingway—who unsenti-
mentally peered into the broken heart of the twentieth
century. The immigrant Church was not innocent of sin
but, a much more serious matter, innocent about poetic
truth. The administrative churchmen who destroyed the
budding intellectual revival at New York's Dunwoodie in
the first decade of the century crushed and exiled the
men who understood the language of myth and symbol
in which the Scriptures had been written. Pope Pius X
crushed the saving poetry of that new age. The immigrant Church was hardheaded and literal, preferring un-
distinguished and sentimental renderings of Catholic
piety to any possibly unsettling invitation to ambiva-

lence in the interpretation of life. It preferred a fluent apologetics to its main business of religious mystery, Fulton Sheen and "Lovely Lady Dressed in Blue" to O'Neill and *Long Day's Journey into Night.*

The criterion for sanctity became a kind of doggedness in doing what was expected, in the "carrying out of the duties of one's state in life." The pattern for such a life of perfection was found in legislation, in correct observance, especially if this demanded sacrifices that went against the deepest and truest instincts of the person's heart. If you didn't like it, it was all the better for your humility and your soul. The template of this driven perfectionism was placed in a thorny crown on the heads of the men and women who gave themselves to the service of the immigrant Church. Docility ranked high among desirable virtues. This was capital punishment for the souls of the perceptive and poetic who, in the meshlike culture, were expected to conform or find themselves guilt-ridden outcasts. Nobody thought it strange that this oppressive perfectionism, which served the institutional Church so well, stood in sharp contrast to the work of the great mystics, such as St. John of the Cross, St. Teresa of Avila, or St. Catherine of Siena, whose spiritual teachings were as profoundly poetic as their own encounters with the Godhead.

Visions, the special province of poets who through them see deeply into history, were reduced to private, mechanical visitations to the supposedly saintly that were often filled with messages of impending doom for the human race. The privatization of religion favored the rise of personal hysterical phenomena that appeared in a dozen confusing guises ranging from the stigmata to the gift of tears, often symptoms of the generalized emotional repression that afflicted Church life rather than authentic indications of holiness. Often the messages that various persons claimed to receive from God were, unlike the genuine revelation of poetry, locked away, as though God kept secrets from the human race instead of prodigally making Himself known, of exuberantly revealing Himself in every richly human experience. Immense and exhausting efforts were made by sincere Catholics who felt that perfection demanded these offerings of themselves to a distant and hard-to-please deity.

The immigrant Church was enormously successful because it emphasized that response so prized by the organizational soul: the dutiful and unquestioning acceptance of centralized authority. The aspiring hierarch's romance with Roman domination came as the nation itself thrilled at reestablishing links to overseas royalty. It was very American, in an elitist sense, to be very European just as the great centralizers, such as William Cardinal O'Connell of Boston, assumed power in the American Church. They closed the poetic era and effectively shut down the possibility of intellectual curiosity among the clergy. It is not surprising that the American Church became such an awesome, obedient, and well-deployed force. Nor is it surprising that it suffered such a long struggle to rediscover near century's end what had been within its grasp at the very beginning. Its enormous achievements were gained at the expense of stifling its deepest sensitivity, of settling for a powerful institution erected on the graves of its poets.

The age of renewal, of course, made it possible for the emotional longings of the immigrant Church to manifest themselves in a number of ways. The Pentecostalism which attracted so many emotionally deprived Catholics, including many priests and religious who had accepted arid lives out of duty, offers an example of how the nonrational, highly vital aspect of religion reasserts itself. Nothing seemed less like well-ordered Catholicism than Pentecostalism. There is, however, a clear linkage. The movement has carefully maintained its relationship with the institutional Church. Its residual obsessiveness is evident in this lingering need for hierarchical approval as well as in the movement's varied demands on its members. This hybrid religious experience permits a controlled freedom of fervor; it even ritualizes its supposedly free-floating prayer forms so that the gift of tongues sounds remarkably the same as it is spoken by most Pentecostals. They are enjoying an emotional religion—religion outside the normal social expression of obsessive, heavily rationalized practice that, since it is always within an environment of control, remains structured even as it allows subjective experiences of a highly charged and energizing nature.

The Pentecostals puzzle the manager bishops of post-immigrant American Catholicism, mainly because they do not know what to do with them. These good people are insistently loyal to the bishops even as they practice a form of prayer that is quite foreign to—and would make distinctly uncomfortable—the typical American bishop. There is, therefore, plenty of room for them in the structure of a Church that would have classified them along with fundamentalist Holy Rollers only a few decades ago.

The Pentecostals give off only a filtered hint about the new order of the universe. Bound to authority, they have not yet looked deeply, as poets must, into the uncharted landscape of contemporary religious life. Now, since the distinction between heaven and earth no longer suffices to support a spiritual awareness, authority cannot be located at the top of things. There is no top of things, no place, literally, that is intrinsically superior to any other in a unified universe. This trackless place may better represent the intuitions of the great poetic spiritual figure who used metaphors of ascent and journey to describe the spiritual quest. St. John of the Cross, speaking of the Mount of Perfection, seems to sigh as he reveals that each must find a unique path to it. That corresponds to the religio-poetic insight of the Arthurian legends which centered on the quest for the Holy Grail. It was the search that was important, and to carry it out each knight found himself standing "at the darkest part of the forest," at a place, in other words, where nobody had cut a path before. That is precisely the religious situation for men and women in the contemporary universe, in the world into which, as on a space ship, we are traveling so swiftly together. The familiar landfalls of the immigrant Church can no longer be seen, authority cannot make authoritarianism work anymore, there is no way there but the way we find ourselves.

The development of the concept of collegiality—of a shared responsibility for the authority even of the hardy, old authority-loving institutional Church—is an example of how, at its most rational, administrative level, the Church has translated impulses that arose deep within itself, in that same infinitely sensitive aspect of its being where it remains vitally in touch with the rhythms of the universe. A collegial Church—in which authoritarianism is operationally recognized as legally and spiritually dead—is to some degree prepared for continued functioning in the radically changed circumstances of the space age. The postimmigrant American Church has a long agenda with which to deal in order to condition itself properly for its continuing journey into the future. The reforms of this future are not, however, the warmed-over enthusiasms of the era of renewal, for these were largely the reworking of themes that were central to the immigrant Church.

The popular election of bishops sounds like a democratic notion when, in reality, it is merely a new rendering of episcopal preeminence that would, in the long run, change nothing. Reforms that concern themselves exclusively with the priesthood emphasize the clerical dominance of American Catholic life that may have been its most severe problem in the heyday of the immigrant Church. Redecorating the old institution simply will not do. The universe is too greatly changed for that. What it demands is what Cardinal Newman called "notional assent" to the implications of our new religious consciousness. For that we can converse with a man, born of Irish Catholic heritage in New York City at the time that the *New York Review* was beginning its enlightened theological speculations at St. Joseph's Seminary at Dunwoodie, New York. In the sweep of his extraordinary life as one of the world's foremost students of mythology, one senses the nature of the religious explorations that are not just for the elect few but for every one of us.

PROPHETS

Called Out of Bondage:
Joseph Campbell on the Religious Consciousness of the Space Age

ALTHOUGH the word is popularly used to denote falsehood, myth is actually a perennial vehicle for expressing truth. Human beings have always told, in mythic forms, the stories they want to be remembered and passed on—such as the Arthurian legends or the enduring biblical tales—to distinguish them from fashions, fads, or the constantly changing facts of almanacs or the Guinness Book of World Records. Myth and symbol are fundamental and essential properties of all religions; they are the special language of religious experience.

Joseph Campbell has devoted his life to their study, detecting recurrent common themes and motifs in the varied mythologies of different cultures that suggest that a single underground spring of religious experience nourishes them all. According to Campbell, what appear to be diverse religious traditions are actually different expressions of a unitary experience that is shared across all cultures.

The author of numerous books on comparative religion and mythology, and a former professor at Sarah Lawrence College in Bronxville, New York, Campbell is perhaps best known for *The Hero with a Thousand Faces*, published in 1949. In this work he traced the stories of ancient and contemporary heroes, showing that their challenges and experiences were essentially the same, that every man was indeed Everyman. The pattern that could be discerned in the timeless stories and symbols of myth could also be discovered in our own lives. As Campbell once told an interviewer, "The latest incarnation of Oedipus, the continued romance of Beauty and the Beast, stand this afternoon at the corner of Forty-second Street and Fifth Avenue, waiting for the light to change."

Campbell's own life parallels that of the mythic hero's journeys and struggles, as he found both the identity and the path of scholarship that were true for him. A New Yorker of Irish Catholic descent who was captivated by Buffalo Bill's Wild West Show as a boy, he began his studies of American Indian culture and experience. Gradually he awakened to the dream of pervasive mythological themes and was called, as he felt within himself, to a long pilgrimage of discovery that led him not only to his own graduate study of the Arthurian romances at Columbia University, but also to European studies of oriental philosophy, religion, and Sanskrit as well as the works of Freud and Jung. In all of these he recognized the common themes that were found in the American Indian culture of his boyhood wonder and the Catholic Church of his boyhood belief.

Kennedy: "Myth" is still a confusing term for many people. Perhaps we could begin by explaining it a little more in detail.

Campbell: Myth has many functions. The first we might term mystical, in that myth makes a connection between our waking consciousness and the whole mystery of the universe. Secondly, myth gives us a map or picture of the universe. That is its cosmological function. It allows us to see ourselves in relationship to nature, as when we speak of Father Sky and Mother Earth. There is also a sociological function for myth, in that it supports and validates a certain social and moral order for us. The story of the Ten Commandments given to Moses by God on Mount Sinai is an example of this. Lastly, myth has a psychological function, in that it offers us a way of passing through, and dealing with, the various stages from birth to death.

Kennedy: You have written of the difficulty of one mythological system's being able to speak to a world which has become so varied. The pastoral agrarian and hunting myths that once spoke to everyone no longer apply quite so easily. But you have also said that, with some reflection, we can understand that the ancient stories of heroes and their adventures are the same as our contemporary search for meaning.

Campbell: Yes, myths come out of the creative imagination we all share, and the story each of us recognizes in our own search for spiritual meaning parallels all the legends of heroes, like the knights of the Round Table, who must travel into an unknown world and do battle with the powers of darkness in order to return with the gift of knowledge.

Kennedy: We are, according to many observers, at a turning point in religious consciousness. That is, the mythological structure—or the legends that undergirded a literal biblical interpretation of the universe—are sharply challenged by the discoveries of the space age.

Campbell: Yes, that is exactly what is happening, with consequences we can all see. One must remember the central truth, for example, about Easter and Passover. We are all called out of the house of bondage, even as the Jews were called out of their bondage in Egypt. We are called out of bondage in the way in which the moon throws off its shadow to emerge anew, in the way that life throws off the shadow of death. Easter and Passover have the same roots; we are called out of bondage to our old tradition. Easter is not Easter and Passover is not Passover unless they release us even from the tradition that gives us these feasts.

Easter and Passover are prime symbols of what we are faced with in the space age. We are challenged both mystically and socially, because our ideas of the universe have been reordered by our experience in space. The consequence is that we can no longer hold onto the religious symbols that we formulated when we thought that the earth was the center of the universe.

Kennedy: You are saying that the perennial power of myth is that it can shed one formulation—such as the pre-Copernican notion of an earth down here and a heaven up there—and yet retain and renew its strength. That means that we are experiencing the mythological truth, in the very challenge to give up the religious understanding of the universe that is very strong in Judeo-Christian imagery. But that the Passover-Easter experience demands that we do that.

Campbell: Easter and Passover make us experience in ourselves a call out of bondage, yes, but so experiencing them does not destroy the religious tradition. Understanding these symbols in their transcendent spiritual sense enables us to see and to possess our religious traditions freshly. The space age demands that we change our ideas about ourselves, but we want to hold onto them. That is why there is a resurgence of old-fashioned orthodoxy in so many areas at the present time. There are no horizons in space, and there can be no horizons on our own experience. We cannot hold onto ourselves and our in-groups as we once did. The space age makes that impossible, but people reject this demand or don't want to think about it. So they pull back into one true church, or black power, or the unions, or the capitalist class.

Kennedy: Then the space age challenges everything that makes us earth-centered or group-centered.

Campbell: Easter and Passover offer the perfect symbols because they mean that we are called to a new life. This new life is not very well defined: that is why we want to hold onto the past. The journey to this new life— and it is a journey we must all make—cannot be made unless we let go of the past. The reality of living in space means that we are born anew, not born again to an old-time religion but to a new order of things. There are no horizons—that is the meaning of the space age. We are in a free fall into a future that is mysterious. It is very fluid and this is disconcerting to many people. All you have to do is know how to use a parachute.

Kennedy: An awareness of mythological truth alerts us to the fact that in the Easter experience we do not just remember historical events but that we are experiencing in ourselves Passover and Easter, that what we feel is the pull of the space age on our own religious consciousness.

Campbell: Yes, we can feel it in ourselves. The space age, which many people want to forget or write off as a bad investment, is central to all this. Almost fifteen years ago we had the great symbol of the change that has taken place. Men stood on the moon and looked back—and by television we were able to look back with them—to see earthrise. That is the symbol that enabled us to feel the truth of the discovery Copernicus made four and a quarter centuries ago. Until then, we may have agreed theoretically with Copernicus but his map of the universe was not available to us, except to mathematicians and astronomers. It was an invisible idea and we could go on thinking, as we did, about an earth down here and a heaven up there, about a religious idea in which everything was divided along the same lines that the heavens and the earth were divided.

Kennedy: If heaven and earth were divided, so too were body and soul, nature and supernature, flesh and spirit. The universe was ordered in a hierarchical fashion and so too were the churches.

Campbell: This divided model allowed us to think that there was a spiritual order, separate or divided from our own experience. Think of how we spoke about things according to that old model. Everything was seen from earthbound eyes. The sun rose and set. Joshua stopped both the sun and the moon to have time to finish a slaughter.

With the moon walk, the religious myth that sustained these notions could no longer be held. With our view of earthrise, we could see that the earth and the heavens were no longer divided but that the earth is in the heavens. There is no division and all the theological notions based on the distinction between the heavens and the earth collapse with that realization. There is a unity in the universe and a unity in our own experience. We can no longer look for a spiritual order outside of our own experience.

Kennedy: That challenges the old ideas that our fate is being decided "out there" by the gods.

Campbell: Or that the stars are their residences, hung with their lanterns. You can still see remnants of that in the disappointment many people feel when our scientific probes do not discover life on Mars.

Kennedy: Isn't it true that Carl Jung once said that the

declaration of the Assumption of the Virgin Mary by the Roman Catholic Church was the most significant religious declaration of this century? Is this a place where we can see the interlocking of literal and symbolic levels of religious statements?

Campbell: Jung did say that and, of course, he was pointing to the profound symbolic, rather than literal, meaning of that doctrine. Literally, it suggests a heaven "up there" to which a body could ascend. But that is a religious doctrine based on a divided notion of the universe. Symbolically, the same tradition suggests that it signifies the return of Mother Earth to the heavens, the very thing that has occurred because of our journeys into space.

Kennedy: Earthrise is a symbol that is working its way slowly into our consciousness. One sees it in many places. CBS News used it for a long time on their evening news. Strangely enough, it has been used—set afire, however—to publicize the movie *The Late Great Planet Earth.* That is a fire-and-brimstone account of the end of the world in literal biblical terms. That use of earthrise seems a good example of the resistance you describe to the space age and its central metaphor.

Campbell: The sense of apocalypse is very widespread and I believe it is a rejection of this new age. That is why there is so much interest in disaster. It's more than just the thrill of the movies. It is evidence of how deep the notion of the apocalyptic moment is. We hate ourselves so much that we take delight in the destruction of people. It is like reading the worst of the prophets in the Bible.

The coming of the second millennium may be accentuating this. We can really expect some of the same things that attended the approach of the year 1000 to occur again. It is in everyone's mind at some level.

We must not understand apocalypse literally, not as some physical destruction and judgment on the world, or as something that is going to occur in the future. The kingdom is here; it does not come through expectation. One looks at the world and sees the radiance. The Easter revelation is right there. We don't have to wait for something to happen. So, in the space age, two themes are evident. First, we must move socially into a new system of symbols, because the old ones do not work. Second, the symbols, as they exist, when they are interpreted spiritually rather than concretely, yield the revelation.

The mystical theme of the space age is this: the world, as we know it, is coming to an end. The world as the center of the universe, the world divided from the heavens, the world bound by horizons in which love is reserved for members of the in-group: that is the world that is passing away. Apocalypse does not point to a fiery Armageddon but to the fact that our ignorance and our complacency are coming to an end. Our divided, schizophrenic world view, with no mythology adequate to coordinate our conscious and unconscious, that is what is coming to an end. The exclusivism of there being only one way in which we can be saved, the idea that there is a single religious group that is in sole possession of the truth, that is the world as we know it that must pass away. What is the kingdom? It lies in our realization of the ubiquity of the divine presence in our neighbors, in our enemies, in all of us.

Kennedy: Much, then, of what we recognize as retrenchment in various religious traditions is a rejection of facing the Easter-Passover demands of passing into the space age?

Campbell: The central demand is to surrender our exclusivity, everything that defines us over against each other. People have used religious affiliations to do this for years. There are two pages in Martin Buber that almost merit his reputation. He speaks of the "I-Thou" and the "I-It" relationships. An ego talking to a *thou* is different from an ego talking to an *it*. Whenever we emphasize otherness or out-groups, we are making persons into *it*. The Gentile, the Jew, the enemy—they all become the same.

Kennedy: What about ethnicity and the emphasis on the search for roots that are so popular these days?

Campbell: It is understandable that people want to search out their roots, especially after all the dislocation and emigration of the last century. Still, an overemphasis on this, understandable though it may be, is a sign of pulling back into in-groups. That is why we see so many movements that are intensely nationalistic or, in recent years in Iran, one that is almost xenophobic, a wish to turn the clock back a thousand years and to reject relationship with any out-group. But our actual ultimate root is in our common humanity, not in our personal genealogy.

Kennedy: The notion of taking one world seriously, despite the awareness we have developed through studying ecology, is still very frightening.

Campbell: It means we have to give up what we know, what we are comfortable with. People draw back to what seems more familiar ground to them.

Kennedy: Is there an explanation here for the fascination with deliverance from powers coming from "out there," whether it is Superman coming from Krypton, or visitors in various spacecraft?

Campbell: It is a clear reflection of an outmoded understanding of the universe, that we will be delivered by some benign visitation, by forces from other planets. It is the idea of the kingdom's coming from a source other than from within ourselves. The kingdom of God is within us but we have this idea that the gods act from "out there."

Kennedy: Is that where we get the impression of unidentified flying objects?

Campbell: It is part of the same thing. As Jung once wrote, unidentified flying objects tell us something of mankind's visionary expectations. People are looking for visits from the outside world. They think our deliverance will come from there, whereas the space age reminds us that it must come from within ourselves. The voyages into outer space turn us back to inner space.

Kennedy: Then films such as *Close Encounters of the Third Kind* are really old-fashioned stories. They don't really tell us about the future.

Campbell: Such a movie is about the past, not the future. It is the idea that we will be visited by friendly forms, that they will come to our aid and save us.

Kennedy: Still, the fact that so many creative persons, so many modern mythmakers, are trying to deal with the impact of space explorations tells us that they feel something in their bones about this change. Do any of these movies capture a sense of what we are talking about?

Campbell: I thought that *2001: A Space Odyssey* was very interesting in the way in which it dealt with symbols. You recall, at the beginning, that we see a community of little manlike apes, Australopithecines, snarling and fighting with each other. But there is one among them who is different, one who is drawn out of curiosity to approach and explore, one who has a sense of awe before the unknown. This one is apart and alone, seated in wonder before a panel of stone standing mysteriously upright in the landscape. He contemplates it, then he reaches out and touches it cautiously, somewhat in the way the first astronaut's foot approached and then gently touched down on the moon. Awe, you see, is what moves us forward. That's what the filmmaker recognized, that there was a continuity through all time of this motivating principle in the evolution of our species. So the panel is seen later on the moon approached by astronauts. And again, floating free in space, mysterious still.

Kennedy: The point is not to argue over the literal symbolism of the slabs but to let them speak to us as symbols. This is what you mean about religious symbols as well.

Campbell: Yes, they do not represent historical facts. A symbol doesn't just point to something else. As Thomas Merton wrote, a symbol contains a structure that awakens our consciousness to a new awareness of the inner meaning of life and reality itself. Through symbols we enter emotionally into contact with our deepest selves, with each other, and with God—a word that is to be understood as a symbol. When theologians spoke of God's being dead, a decade or so ago, just as the space age began, they were really saying that their symbols were dead.

Kennedy: You see a distinction between religion based on the literal interpretation of symbols as historical events and one in which the symbols are mystical references that help us see into ourselves.

Campbell: Yes, the latter is the religion of mysticism, the other a religion of belief in concrete objects, God as a concrete object. In order to understand a concrete symbol we have to let go of it. When you can let the literal meaning of a religious tradition die, then it comes alive again. And this also frees you to respect other religious traditions more. You don't have to be afraid of losing something when you let go of your tradition.

Kennedy: Isn't something like this actually happening in some religious bodies? In the Roman Catholic Church, for example, many people no longer readily accept the authority of the clergy to regulate their lives, but at the same time they discover that they are close to and even like their Catholic tradition. They seem to possess it in a new way.

Campbell: Yes, that is happening in various groups. Many people have learned to let religious symbols speak directly to themselves to order their lives. They don't believe that a group of bishops or other religious leaders could meet in conference and decide for them which interpretation of a symbol must be believed. But they don't reject their religious tradition. They discover that symbols, when they are not pressed literally, can speak clearly across different traditions. The churches have to ask themselves: Are we going to emphasize the historical Christ, or the second person of the Blessed Trinity, the one who knows the Father? If you emphasize the historical, you deemphasize the spiritual power that is the symbol of the basic consciousness that is within us.

Kennedy: Isn't it disconcerting for a person to reexamine his or her own religious tradition that way?

Campbell: Yes, that is the problem of letting the tradition die. The mystical writer Meister Eckhart once wrote that the ultimate leave-taking is the leaving of God for God. People feel panicky at the thought that we might all have something in common, that they are giving up some exclusive hold on the truth. It is something like discovering that you are a Frenchman and a human being at the same time. That is exactly the challenge that the great religions face in the space age.

Kennedy: So, in this free fall into the future, understanding our religious symbols is a way of using our parachutes. What about symbols in religious worship?

Campbell: Well, they are meant to be respected, but often they are not. Preachers think they have to explain them instead of letting them speak for themselves. That is why the destruction of the Catholic liturgy in the name of reform was such a disaster. It was an effort to make ancient symbols and rituals more rational. And they threw out the Gregorian chant and other great symbolic achievements in the process; they disowned religious symbols that spoke directly to people without need of mediation. The old ritual of the mass spoke powerfully to people. Now the celebrant carries out a Julia Child sort of function at the altar.

Kennedy: The justification was that it was the reasonable thing to do. But worship is not reasonable in that sense. You have written that part of our loss of a sense of meaning, our "wasteland" experience, is due to the fact that we have lost our connections with a mythical understanding of our lives.

Campbell: The problem has been that institutionalized religions have not allowed symbols to speak directly to people in their proper sense. Religious traditions translate mythological signs into references to historical events, whereas properly they stem from the human imagination and speak back to the psyche. Historical events are given spiritual meaning by being interpreted mythologically, for instance, with virgin births, resurrections, and miraculous passages of the Red Sea. When you translate the Bible with excessive literalism, you demythologize it. The possibility of a convincing reference to the individual's own spiritual experience is lost.

Kennedy: How would you define mythology here?

Campbell: My favorite definition of mythology: other people's religion. My favorite definition of religion: misunderstanding of mythology. The misunderstanding consists in the reading of the spiritual mythological symbols as though they were primarily references to historical events. Localized provincial readings separate the various religious communities. Remythologization—recapturing the mythological meaning—reveals a common spirituality of mankind. At Easter, to return to our example, we might suggest the renewal of the knowledge of our general human spiritual life through casting off, for a moment, our various historical concretizations.

Kennedy: Remythologization would rescue the stories of the Bible, then, from historical literalism and a susceptibility to debunking. Can we connect that with the example of the Easter experience? What of the cross and the crucifixion?

Campbell: If we think of the crucifixion only in historical terms we lose the reference of the symbol immediately to ourselves. Jesus left his mortal body on the cross, the sign of earth, to go to the Father with whom he was one. We, similarly, are to identify with the eternal life that is within us. The symbol at the same time tells us of God's willing acceptance of the cross—that is to say, participation in the trials and sorrows of human life in the world. So that He is here within us—not by way of a fall or a mistake, but with rapture and joy. Thus the cross has a dual sense—one, our going to the divine, and the other, the coming of the divine to us. It is a true crossing.

Kennedy: What about the symbols of Easter and Passover? How would one, as you have said, let go of these in order to possess them anew in this first generation of the space age?

Campbell: What has always been basic to resurrection, or Easter, is crucifixion. If you want to resurrect, you must have crucifixion. Too many interpretations of the crucifixion have failed to emphasize that. They emphasize the calamity of the event. And if you emphasize calamity, then you look for someone to blame. That is why people have blamed the Jews for it. But it is not a calamity if it leads to new life. Through the crucifixion we were unshelled, we were able to be born to resurrection. That is not a calamity. We must look freshly at this so that its symbolism can be sensed.

St. Augustine speaks of going to the cross as a bridegroom to his bride. There is an affirmation here. In the Prado there is a great painting by Titian of Simon of Cyrene as he willingly helps Jesus with the cross. The picture captures the human participation, the free, voluntary participation we all must have in the Easter-Passover mystery.

Kennedy: So one must step out of one's tradition to see it clearly again.

Campbell: That is what we are challenged to do. Self-preservation is only the second law of life. The first law is that you and the other are one. Politicians love to talk about "I worship in my way, and he in his." But that doesn't make sense if we are one with each other. That is the truth the space age urges on us, but many religious institutions resist it.

Kennedy: Perhaps we can explore the Easter-Passover symbolism in more detail. These feasts, calculated according to the full moon, share much in common.

Campbell: Here we face very similar themes in the Jewish and Christian traditions. The theme is also found in the mystery religions in which Adonis dies and is resurrected.

Kennedy: And all these come at springtime, matching the bursting forth of flowers and the return of the sun. Even the plangent longing we experience at this season must be related to this.

Campbell: Yes, it is very much the longing to be born anew the way nature is. All these elements fit together. Easter is calculated as the Sunday that follows the first full moon after the vernal equinox. It is evidence of a concern centuries before Christ to coordinate the lunar and solar calendars. What we have to recognize is that these celestial bodies represented to the ancients two different modes of eternal life, one engaged in the field of time, life throwing off death, as the moon its shadow, to be born again; the other, disengaged and eternal. The dating of Easter according to both lunar and solar calendars suggests that life, like the light that is reborn in the moon and eternal in the sun, finally is one.

Kennedy: What of some of the folk symbols of Easter and Passover? Do they all have similar lunar and solar resonations?

Campbell: There is, to begin with, the rabbit, the Easter bunny. Many peoples of the world see a rabbit in the shadows of the moon. The rabbit is associated with the dying and the resurrection of the moon. The egg is shelled off by the chick as the shadow of the moon is by the moon reborn, or as slough by the serpent reborn. So the chick from the egg is another sign of the birth of the spirit at Easter.

Birds in flight are symbolic of the spirit released from the bondage of earth. So the moon rabbit, the cast-off eggshell, and the just-born bird that is to fly give us together a playful, childlike reading of the Easter message.

*   *   *

It has drawn on in the day as Campbell, with the broad grin of an Irish cop, returns to his reflections about space. The walls of the apartment seem to slide away like a roof of a planetarium and he stands, a boy from the sidewalks of New York who watched Glenn Curtiss' first wobbly plane flight above Riverside Drive almost more than seventy years ago, Merlin standing with a pointer at the gates of the cosmos.

Campbell: The problem is that people have tried to look away from space and from the meaning of the moon landing. I remember seeing a picture of an astronaut standing on the moon. It was up at Yale and someone had scrawled on it, "So what?" That is the arrogance of the kind of academic narrowness one too often sees; it is trapped in its own predictable prejudices, its own stale categories. It is the mind dulled to the poetry of existence. It's fashionable now to demand some economic payoff from space, some reward to prove it was all worthwhile. Those who say this resemble the apelike creatures in *2001*. They are fighting for food among themselves, while one separates himself from them and moves to the slab, motivated by awe. That is the point they are missing. He is the one who evolves into a human being: he is the one who understands the future.

There have been budget cutbacks in the space program. We shrug it off. But that is where we live. It is not "out there." And the great symbol remains, that remarkable view of earthrise. Earthrise is like all symbols. They resemble compasses. One point is in a fixed place but the other moves to the unknown. The fear of the unknown, this free fall into the future, can be detected all around us. But we live in the stars and we are finally moved by awe to our greatest adventures. The kingdom of God is within us. Easter and Passover, particularly, remind us that we have to let go in order to enter it.

Theologian for the Now and Future Church— Karl Rahner

IN MARCH 1979 a white-haired German Jesuit named Karl Rahner arrived in New York from Munich as inconspicuously as a pensioned-off civil servant en route to visit relatives in Milwaukee. In fact, Karl Rahner made his way to that city to attend a theological symposium at Marquette University honoring him on his seventy-fifth birthday. He hitched a ride there from Chicago with a young Jesuit theologian in an aging, mud-splattered car, and he stayed at his destination in a sparely furnished room with a bath down the hall.

If this pilgrim's progress attracted little attention outside the highly specialized world of theology, Rahner's quiet lifetime of work had already profoundly affected the Roman Catholic Church's self-understanding and pastoral practice. Indeed, this unassuming priest, the private man in the ill-fitting business suit cupping his ear to listen to the delivery of a seminar paper, may prove to be a more pervasive and enduring influence on the Church than that most public and charismatic of figures, Pope John Paul II.

"Compared to Karl Rahner, most other contemporary Christian theologians are scrub oak," that was the judgment of Dr. Martin E. Marty, professor of the history of modern Christianity at the University of Chicago, as he cited a poll in which 554 North American theologians from 71 different denominations named Rahner—after Paul Tillich and St. Thomas Aquinas—as the greatest influence on their work. Although Rahner placed ahead of even Martin Luther and St. Augustine, well-read Americans who have at least a cocktail-conversation familiarity with twentieth-century theologians such as Tillich, Reinhold Niebuhr, and Karl Barth seem never to have heard of him. But if Rahner has avoided celebrity in an age that feasts on it, his work has inspired bold and highly publicized themes. These include the so-called "theology of liberation," which has fused religious idealism with political action in the Third World to thrust priests and bishops to the forefront of social reform movements. Rahner has also provided a firm theoretical foundation for the doctrine of collegiality, which acknowledges the bishops' independent claim to ecclesiastical authority, drastically and permanently reordering the monarchical model of the papacy and making the bishops working partners with the Pope in governing the Church. In short, a theologian for a new age.

The old Jesuit's impact has been primarily on professional theologians, but they in turn have multiplied Rahner's influence by transmitting it in universities and seminaries to a generation of priests and ministers who speak directly to Christian assemblies in pulpits and classrooms throughout the world. He has remained at his desk for most of the last forty years, shunning the fame achieved by some of the younger theologians he has influenced, such as Swiss scholar Hans Küng. Slightly stooped and as reserved as an old field marshal, Rahner has produced some 3,500 books and articles in his primary bibliography, providing the most thorough and systematic treatment of theological topics since the famous thirteenth-century *Summa* of Aquinas. His has been a massive and intense effort to express the ancient dogmas of Catholicism in an idiom that can be spoken and understood in contemporary culture, and the phantom quality of his presence has only increased his intellectual influence, which, in some ways, resembles that of a double agent in the Roman Catholic Church. On the one hand, he has been a loyal son of the Church who has never believed in throwing out even the driest husks of traditional Catholic teaching and practice; instead, Rahner reexamines them to see if living cells still exist that can be scraped free and replanted in the soil of the modern world. On the other hand, once Rahner has established this continuity between the past and the present, he is a philosophical Burbank of mutations and permutations, giving birth to blooms of thought that appear radically transformed.

A clear example of Rahner's technique of retrieval and restatement may be found in the address he wrote that a former student of his translated and delivered in English at a Congregational church in Cambridge, Massachusetts, when he received an honorary degree from the Weston School of Theology in 1979. In his typical fashion, Rahner began with the declarations of the Second Vatican Council, at which he played a significant role as a theological expert. In these authoritative documents he found evidence for a further ecclesiastical transformation that he described as "a leap to a world church."

Specifically citing the shift from Latin to the vernacular mass legislated by the bishops at the council, he noted, "The victory of the vernacular in the Church's liturgy signals unmistakably the becoming of a world church whose individual churches exist independently in their respective cultural spheres, inculturated, and no longer a European export."

The congregations of the Roman Curia, Rahner continued, "still have the mentality of a centralistic bureaucracy which considers itself to know best what serves the kingdom of God and souls in all the world, and takes the mentality of Rome or Italy as its standard in a frighteningly naive way."

If such attacks on an ingrown Roman officialdom are familiar, they have seldom been uttered by a man more difficult for the Curia to censure or assail. For the consciousness of the wider Church has been thoroughly seeded, as if with timed-release pills, by Rahner's ideas and methodology. Perhaps that is why Pope John Paul II, whose own theological education was broken off before Rahner's influence heightened in the 1950s, seemed somewhat cool and unenthusiastic about the Jesuit's work, according to a close theological colleague, when the Pontiff and Rahner met a few months after the Pope was elected in 1978.

Indeed, the contrast between the old theologian and Pope John Paul II symbolizes the conflict, obscured by John Paul's winning instincts for public relations, that rumbles like a shifting geological fault beneath the Catholic Church. No thinker has shown more respect for ecclesiastical authority than Rahner, yet few have pressed so hard to open it to reexamination and reformulation in the modern world.

The Pope would have been further amazed by what Rahner said next in Cambridge. In the form of a rhetorical question, Rahner directly challenged Roman—indeed, even Western—dominance of moral thinking. "Must the marital morality of the Masai in East Africa be that of Western Christianity?" he asked. "Or could a chieftain there, even if he is a Christian, live in the style of the patriarch Abraham?"

The suggestion that Catholicism must respect cultural traditions to the extent of condoning an African's having many wives was, of course, merely a symbol of Rahner's vision of the vastly transformed Church of the future, and a prime example of his theological method, which taxis steadily along on unassailable Church documents, like Lindbergh's plane on the flats of Roosevelt Field, until suddenly it takes flight in a wobbly arc that changes history.

*   *   *

Rahner's achievement has been to modernize Catholic theological reflection and to make it intellectually respectable again. While others, notably his fellow Jesuit, Canadian Bernard Lonergan, have also contributed enormously, Rahner has clearly been the single most important figure in shaping current theological attitudes and methods. He has not only brought Catholic theology down from the clouds of self-contained and self-assured speculation about the heritage of Thomas Aquinas, but he has also attempted to listen to the questions posed by the contemporary world, straining, with the almost numbing capacity of a Germanic scholar for extracting details from a situation, to understand the potentially religious motives and needs of even those who proclaim the death of God and the irrelevance of faith.

Rahner coined the term "anonymous Christian" to describe those people whom he identified as possessing a

genuine religious spirit even though they might profess
other faiths or, seemingly, no faith at all. While supporting the Catholic Church's right to proclaim its faith ex-
plicitly, Rahner has consistently described a vision of the
universe in which all men and women ultimately will be
saved by a loving God who is beyond our comprehen-
sion.

"An orthodox theologian," Rahner says dryly, "is forbidden to teach that everybody will be saved. But we are
allowed to *hope* that all will be saved. If I hope to be
saved, it is necessary to hope that for all men as well. If
you have reason to love another, you can hope that all
will be saved."

That Rahner has succeeded in developing what has
been termed transcendental Thomism—that is, in bring-
ing theology back to a base in human historical experience—is the more remarkable in light of the Catholic
Church's determined battle, earlier in the century,
against contemporary intellectual inquiry. Catholic his-
torians count the changing of the guard at St. Joseph's
Seminary at Dunwoodie as symbolic of the beginning of
the era of closed, tightly disciplined seminary life that
was to last for the next fifty years. The theology of St.
Thomas was the only acceptable formula in American
seminaries and it was quickly boxed into a tight set of
apologetic propositions.

Tragically enough, the "perpendicular Gothic," as it
has been called, of Thomism was never meant to be a
closed system of thought. It was, in fact, a synthesis that
vindicated the peaceful coexistence of the realms of faith
and reason. Reformulating Church doctrine in Aristote-
lian terms, Aquinas celebrated the activity of the intellect through which man sought knowledge of the world
and God. Unfortunately, Aquinas' system came to be
applied rigidly and defensively by Church administra-

tors who saw it as the sole admissible mode of reflection on the perplexing mysteries of existence. Ossified Thomism was a bulwark of the rigidly disciplined and pervasively anti-intellectual seminaries of the American immigrant Church. Before Vatican II, textbooks of theology were compendiums of truths established and errors refuted by the diligent application of St. Thomas' principles. Thus armed, the clergy set out to judge rather than to engage in dialogue with their society. This use of his work would have horrified Aquinas since it provided all the answers and left no room for new questions.

"Theology," John Updike has written, "is not a provable accumulation, like science, nor is it a suggestion of enduring monuments, like art. It must always unravel and be reknit." Rahner, who was influenced by the German existentialist philosopher Martin Heidegger, began reknitting Catholic theology when, as a young priest, he was assigned to the Jesuit theological faculty at Innsbruck, Austria, just before the Second World War. He had already known his share of intellectual difficulties, because his doctoral thesis on "Spirit in the World" had originally been rejected by a long-forgotten professor at the University of Freiburg on the grounds that it did not accurately represent the teaching of St. Thomas. At Innsbruck, Rahner began to reflect on the classic themes of Christian spirituality, such as "grace," in the light of existentialism's concern with the urgency of man's ethical choices in his relationship to God.

When the Nazis disbanded the theological faculty, Rahner was sent to Vienna, where he spent the war years doing pastoral work and some occasional lecturing. It was only after the war, in the fragile renaissance of Catholic theological reflection pioneered by Jean Danielou and Henri de Lubac in France, that Rahner was to embark on his major investigations of traditional teachings. Into a theological world of numberless clear propositions and distinctions, a world that defined heaven in terms of a glistening Cartesian concept of a beatific vision of transparent intellectual purity ("I am in heaven, therefore I see"), Rahner reintroduced ambiguity, speaking of God as pure mystery and rescuing the mysterious as a proper quality of religious experience.

Rahner has continually insisted on retrieving not the final, convincing rational explanation for God that was supposedly contained in Aquinas' five proofs of His existence, but the shadowed core of existence, conserving mystery and alerting people to its constant presence. Shaking his head at those who feel that they can explain everything with theological principles, he says, "You shouldn't explain, but show that you cannot explain everything. The theologian reduces everything to God and explains God as unexplainable. Christianity intensifies our experience of mystery; it makes us more aware of it; it makes the mysterious more absolute. Christianity makes demands on mankind and prepares us for the acceptance of mystery." This is the central theme of Rahner's theological reflections.

As David Tracy, a leading Catholic theologian, has said, "Mystery was always a word with either spooky or problem-oriented overtones. In the Catholic tradition, scholars would come to some point where things could not be linked up or where contradictions loomed and they would say, 'And that is where the mystery is.' Protestant theologians, looking at the same problems, would say, 'That is the stumbling block that is the test of true belief'—or, in their popular phrase, 'the scandal of faith.' Rahner broke through because he understood that there is no place in existence where there isn't mystery. Mystery is a quality that inheres in and is indispensable to our existence."

Faith, then, in Rahner's formulation, is not comfort derived from the acceptance of a rote religious formula but an opening of oneself to the fact that we cannot explain the mystery that is a vital rather than an alien aspect of existence.

In effect, Rahner has turned theologians away from the certainty and clarity of doctrine and exposition that dominated Catholic scholastic theology for centuries and directed them toward ambiguity that would delight a poet. He has profoundly shifted the center of gravity of the Catholic Church's teaching function. Rahner says that the Church, even in gatherings such as ecumenical councils in which it proposes to be definitive, does not speak the last word, not even on its understanding of Jesus Christ. He emphasizes how little we know theologically, speaking of our knowledge as a scattering of islands in a vast unknown ocean. He insists that theologians cannot make existence more clear, but that they can create a greater appreciation of its complexity.

An exact reflection of Rahner's approach may be found in a few sentences in his book, *Foundations of Christian Faith.* "Today, too, Christology has an urgent task. A task which is not accomplished by merely repeating literally the ancient formulas and their explanation. . . . Neither can this task consist in abolishing the ancient formulas. But it is an urgent necessity that we broaden the horizons, the modes of expression and the different aspects for expressing the ancient Christian dogmas." A new era of more modest and mystagogic teaching lies before the bishops of the Roman Catholic Church, although many of them have yet to realize or understand this.

*   *   *

Rahner moves rapidly, like a slightly off-balance shore bird hurrying along the sea's edge, darting forward with a poke here or a tug there, making constant inspections, which, though brief, apparently satisfy his curiosity about things, about inanimate objects of all kinds—pushing buttons on water fountains, opening panels marked "Fire Extinguisher," testing and probing but discovering nothing as tangible or final as a morsel of food that rewards the bird's search. There is no final consummatory delight, only more exploration, a feeling for the texture of an object, a cock of the head, a pronunciation half aloud of the words on a street sign or a brand name on a billboard. Bundled in a gray, bone-buttoned overcoat too large for him, this compassionate man is constantly distracted by the shapes and sizes of the material world around him; there is something boyish about him, the good son in the steel-rimmed glasses who always did his lessons well.

His open face turns as sharp and serious as a hanging judge's, however, when he begins to speak about a theological point that he wishes to clarify. He balks at being compared to Einstein, who also came from the Black Forest section of Germany, but not because he disdains the role of great man. "Einstein," he says animatedly, "was from the other side of the mountain." Jabbing the air with a stubby finger, he goes on. "Besides, what was of peripheral concern for Einstein is a central concern for Christians. The mystery bothered him, the mystery of the universe. He tried but he could not explain it." Then Rahner pauses, his eyes suddenly twinkling. "The mystery of the universe, the mystery that cannot be explained, that is what attracts me."

Rahner reveals very little directly about himself. As he briefly recounts his life in German, he speaks of no relationships outside of his family that seem to have been either close or significant in shaping his character or thought. When asked about major influences in his early work, he answers almost curtly, like a commander giving a routine order, "There were none. There were no great figures at that time." He speaks matter-of-factly, like a man who has gone through many interviews, about his family. The son of a high school teacher, he was the middle child of seven siblings, five boys and two girls. Two brothers became doctors, while another, Hugo, also became a Jesuit and a theologian. This modern theologian seems almost nostalgic for a long-gone world as he says proudly, "We never owned a car of our own." His mother, whom he describes as having been very religious, died in her hundred and first year in 1976. He seems detached rather than aloof, determined to keep his personal life to himself.

"The work of the theologian is scholarly reflection on the beliefs and proclamations of Christianity through the Church." He waits only a moment, as though he expected the next question. "And if you ask why this is useful, why is anything useful or of profit? It is more important than something you can buy for money, just as a Beethoven symphony is. Even if not useful economically, theology has significance for life. If you ask, first of all, for usefulness, then you have failed to grasp the essence of theology. It asks about basic, originating questions, about the whole of reality. It is concerned with all of existence in the original unity of all, the ground of reality. Theology touches upon all subjects."

By just such a definition, Rahner has made theology address every aspect of human experience, pulling it back from the specialized concerns and other-worldly categories that dominated it for centuries. Underscoring his belief that "all life is the subject matter for theological reflection," he has written theological meditations on the most ordinary experiences, such as sleeping and waking up, or eating a meal. He even produced an essay on the Beatles, noting that a theologian who wants to understand the world must listen to popular music.

It is partly due to the omnivorous nature of Rahner's interests that his influence has been so widespread. The development of what is known as the "theology of liberation" rests in part on Rahner's theological anthropology —that is, his readiness to relate Christianity to individual experience. The old scholasticism provided answers to cover any situation without being responsive to particular events or problems. But Rahner's transcendental Thomism allows one to theologize about situations as concrete as the distended bellies of undernourished children, and to transform theology itself with the answers.

*   *   *

Rahner is a man who observes the world not to indict it as a wrathful prophet but to understand it as a wise old therapist. "The theologian thinks not only for himself," he says, "but also for others. If a man stands before God, he gets anxious if he doesn't conceive of this absolute mystery as absolutely loving and reconciling." He pauses. "The modern theologian tries mostly to exonerate the human person, to unburden him. He is concerned about man as a subject with freedom and responsibility before the mystery of God."

Rahner comes to the edge of irritation when it is suggested that many people do not feel that theologians actually carry out the function he describes. "That is a false reproach," he counters vigorously. "So much the worse for you if you do not ask the questions that theologians do. Theology is like Einstein's theory. You cannot say that abstractions do not touch you. These abstractions need mediation, however, and every theologian must try to mediate between his specialized language and the many languages of today's world.

"There is missing today," Rahner says, "a spirituality which is deep and which speaks to normal human beings. Those in such movements as the charismatics and others may be a bit socially frustrated—I suspect that this is so. Such movements are not for the average person; they are generally somewhat marginal in society, made up of people who do not find it easy to be part of the larger group.

"As to the Church, it is still a good question to ask how far Christianity needs a specific and spectacular presence. The answer is not necessarily positive. One could imagine God's Providence requiring that only a small part of mankind be specifically spiritual. The Church is not so much something you have to join; it is linked with salvation, but how the Christian sign is to be manifested in the human race only God knows. One could really ask if Christianity were not still somewhat anonymous. In fact, it can be found in an anonymous way in all humanitarian trends. Things that are humane are basically Christian.

"And clearly there will be new religions, most of five or six years' duration. Things like the excitement about Zen and so forth; these are all fads and won't become more than that. I am hopeful, without being a *Dummkopf*, of being able to believe in the future of the Church. Perhaps it will be only a small group that presents itself as proclaiming the possibility of salvation. This would confirm God's plan in history."

Rahner obviously anticipates a Church whose practices will be greatly modified in the future. As it grows more truly universal and is dominated less by Italian administrators, it will, in his vision, solve problems that now seem pressing simply by outgrowing them. He does not believe that a celibate priesthood will survive as the shortage of priests grows. Nor does he think that celibacy or the refusal to ordain women can be defended on theological grounds. "You have to make a distinction between dogmatic teaching and ecclesiastical discipline," he says.

Rahner smiles slightly. "Nobody says the Church in its development in this world will have to look the same as it does now." He pauses; then, in a typical conclusion, adds, "The Pope might move to the Philippines and have good reason to do so. Who knows? That may make more sense geographically."

What about papal leadership, a questioner wants to know, and what expectations does Rahner have of Pope John Paul II? "We can hope now that the Pope will serve in his office well. But we should not expect everything innovative and creative from the Pope. In history, most innovations have come from individuals other than the Pope. Look at St. Francis of Assisi, for example, or St. Catherine of Siena. We have had no great theology from a Pope since Leo the Great. If popes provide us with inspiration, that is fine, but there are many other Christians we can rely on." Rahner emphasizes that an essential task of future theology will be to make it clear that the Church's authority does not reside solely in the Pope but is shared among the bishops.

For those who think that theorists do not affect history, the image of Karl Marx bent over his books in the British Museum may serve as a chastening reminder. Rahner is not a man to incite rebellion in the Catholic Church, but he has certainly provided the theological underpinnings for transformations that he feels are inevitable.

Rahner's effect on the Church flows, in some measure at least, from the fact that he and the rising generation of theologians he has inspired do not set out to deal specifically with matters of internal concern to the Church but rather with the large questions that plague the whole human race. The pressure exerted by theologizing on these issues will incidentally trigger many transformations in the Catholic Church. In a sense, theologians are causing change by making the Church look at the world instead of only at itself.

What, then, is the most important question for theologians? "In the end," Rahner says, "there is one question: Is human existence absurd, or does it possess comprehensive, ultimate meaning? The theologian, the person with faith, says there is ultimate significance. The serious writer always has an implicit theology. The poet asks these questions, Dostoyevsky and Camus ask the same questions. Theology asks them at a deeper level, trying to get to the original evocation of the relationship between God and human beings. This is a human task, and theology does it in its own language so that people can understand something of it in their own language. If people are hungry for meaning, that is a result of the existence of God. If God does not exist, the hunger is absurd. The hunger is a longing that cannot be satisfied. A desire for God presumes the existence of God. If you have a longing for a mountain of gold, that may or may not be satisfied. But a longing for God cannot be taken away. Man is a being who does not live absurdly because he loves, because he hopes, and because God, the holy mystery, is infinitely receptive and acceptant of him."

The Popes of Transition

THE PAPACY retains a unique power over the world's imagination as the most effective of religious offices. The immigrant Church of this century, largely under the influence of cardinal princes who were intoxicated with *Romanità*, came to equate loyalty to the Pope with a profession of their faith. As the late Cardinal Cody said to a theologian whose critique of infallibility rankled him, "The kind of Irish I am, when somebody insults the Pope, you come out fighting." The successor of Peter symbolizes the Church's lineage and identity as well as its tradition and stability. The Pope reminds the Church of its origins but is also responsible for shepherding it into the future. Processing history as though it were timeless is one of the Pope's great symbolic chores. The century began with a Holy Father who, flexing his infallibility, closed the Church to new learning, a move that has been largely, if carefully and gradually, undone by those who followed him. The difficulty in carrying out such maneuvers illustrates the strength and weakness of the papal position. Whoever is Pope must respect his predecessors and, even while effectively nullifying their work, must make it appear that he is merely extending their historical insight. The central requirement for a Pope is not great administrative ability but a genius for the pastoral art.

The most potent element in the pastoral art is the adroit fashioning of symbols. These, in shorthand, communicate the tone, meaning, and direction of the Pope and the Church. Far more significantly than most of a Pope's written words are his gestures, the moves through which his values and commitments are revealed to the world. Pope John XXIII, for example, followed comfortable instincts that put the world at ease with him as well as with his office, which for twenty years under Pius XII had seemed remote and imperial. Nobody recalls the encyclical John wrote, reinstating Latin as the language of seminary training. The world, profoundly moved by his death, responded with an unprecedented show of symbols. Everywhere non-Catholic churches draped themselves in mourning. This was a sign of the completed symbolic circle of John's communication with the world.

John well understood that although he could institute changes—and he had trouble enough from within curial ranks even doing that—seeing them through would be another matter. It was no small symbol when he sent Milan's Archbishop Giovanni Montini the white typewriter that had been used by Pius XI, no small gesture that, in making him a cardinal, he referred to him as his *prima creatura.* He was, in fact, placing Montini in a position to succeed him, judging him to possess the intelligence, skills, and ecclesiastical experience to carry through the *aggiornamento* which he had initiated. Paul VI lived through fifteen difficult years, the heart of the

Vatican transition, and may finally be perceived as the most extraordinary Pope of the century. He understood that transforming an institution like the Catholic Church was the most delicate of tasks. It demanded the exhausting pastoral art of encouraging change while holding it steady at the same time, something like giving a haircut to a drowsy lion.

Pope John Paul II, who so robustly fills the stage of our consciousness with his confidence and certitude, may lead us to look with a surprising appreciation at the late Pope who, even as he preached to the world, seemed to stand half shadowed by its ambiguity and anguish. Paul, who seemed hardly mourned and quickly forgotten, rises again in our imagination like the memory of a relative who may not have been as distant or eccentric as we once thought. In death Paul VI, written off by extremists on both sides during the struggles of renewal, is receiving more sympathetic attention than he ever did during his lifetime.

That tendency has not been accepted uncritically by those who still perceive *Humanae Vitae* as the tragic centerpiece of his papacy. Still there is a fresh admiration for what Paul did accomplish as well as for the scope of his unprecedented risks against enormous opposition in leading the Church into modern times.

That he failed in many areas is, in the judgment of many, not as significant as his successes. And, perhaps the most redeeming characteristic of all, he is now remembered as utterly human, a man as flawed as any Christian believer, who could weep at the sacrifice and pain he knew were the consequences of his unyielding positions.

Aware that permanently damaging schisms often followed movements toward inner Church transformations, Paul, with the optimistic expectations of liberals weighing heavily upon him, chose a course that not only disappointed them but that also alienated conservatives who felt that he had clouded the imperial identity of the Roman Church. But he held to his convictions. The warmth observed by those who encountered him close up hardly ever softened the image of a fierce gray-eyed eagle who clung to his centrist perch through a long twilight of frailty when he could no longer soar. He seemed, indeed, slowly to fade rather than to die, to become wraithlike and then to disappear quietly from a world that was not as filled with hope as he had once supposed.

Perhaps no document of the Second Vatican Council was more significant than *The Church in the Modern World*, which breathed a new spirit of sensitivity to human experience and a willingness to monitor the world's rhythmic groans and its troubled efforts to pursue a destiny inextricably connected with redemption and salvation. Pope Paul VI, with a world view strongly affected by French thinkers such as Jacques Maritain and Jean Guitton, seemed to appreciate the contemporary world and to view it, not as a pagan marketplace to be shunned, but as the garden after the fall, the setting for all faulted human endeavor in which the Church should always be present. He was a sophisticated and modern Pope, a man whose very choice of a name symbolized his sense of commitment to a world beyond the Church's walls. It was no surprise that his first journey out of Rome, in itself a dramatic sign of reentry into worldly affairs, was to visit the Patriarch Athenagoras, thus ending a break in official relationships with the Orthodox Church that had lasted for five hundred years.

So Paul continued to explore the world, retiring forever the notion of the Pope as "the prisoner of the Vatican," the half-proud, half-self-pitying description that had been applied to pontiffs ever since their earthly kingdom had shrunk a hundred years before to their walled dominion within Rome. If he were not so bold in his moves within the Church—if, in other words, he failed to make the dramatic changes that were pressed upon him by the self-styled progressives who identified him as their natural leader—Paul was still committed to reform but in a step-wise symbolic fashion that would not shatter the papacy's authority or the Church's structural integrity. There were, therefore, no outright repudiations of the traditions which were deeply ingrained in the Catholic consciousness; Paul did not modify celibacy for priests or (despite the recommendation of the study commission he appointed) indicate a willingness to change the Church's teaching about birth control. Paul followed his own diplomat's intuition about the style of change that was possible without destroying the Church.

His practice of the pastoral art, too subtle by half for many, was to maintain the major elements of tradition while permitting the controlled infusion of new ideas. He would not do away with ancient instruments and symbols but he would enrich and revivify them so that they would better serve the Church in the short run and lead to greater reform in the long run.

The college of cardinals provides a good example. In the clamor for renovation after the close of Vatican II, many suggested that the notion of the cardinalate could safely be retired. Who, after all, needed princes in a Church that was shaking off its imperial style?

No gesture allows us to understand Paul more clearly than his refusal to abandon the college of cardinals. Instead he chose to transform it into a gathering of prelates who would truly reflect the Church's international character. He expanded its membership, in one stroke permanently breaking the traditional Italian domination of its ranks and sending red hats to sections of the world that had never before been represented. In more than token numbers cardinals were named from Africa, the Far East, and the Pacific islands. Paul made the college of cardinals a truly symbolic gathering of prelates, a mixture of races, colors, and traditions that was authentically catholic.

Nor was he yet finished. Against enormous opposition within the Roman Curia, he went further than anyone would have predicted in assuring that the college would be able to exercise its power and balance the veteran Italian bureaucrats who had run the Church for so long. Just as Paul diminished something of the pomp and worldly splendor of the cardinalate at each of his consistories, snipping off lengthy trains here and yards of watered red silk there, he also took away the vote of all college members who were over the age of eighty.

This was a deft counterpoint to his demand that bishops turn in their resignations when they reached seventy-five. Taking away a cardinal's crimson shoes and red galerum was one thing, but taking away his pragmatic political power was quite another. Paul VI was no vacillating Hamlet as he effected these changes; he was a determined man who wished to hurt nobody's feelings but who nevertheless moved to remake the college of cardinals into a universal body whose power no longer lay solely in Italian hands.

While John Paul II has become a superstar on the stage of international relations, it is doubtful that he would have moved into that position so easily without the subtle preparatory work of Paul VI. The latter Pope greatly expanded the Holy See's openness to the world, doubling, within the first ten years of his reign, the number of countries, mostly non-Western and non-Christian, with whom the Vatican had diplomatic relations. His emphasized closer contacts with Communist countries, applauding the United States' recognition of mainland China as a sign of hope, a proof of "something new . . . happening in the world." The various diplomatic initiatives which improved the lot of Catholics behind the Iron Curtain would hardly have been possible had Paul not personally approved in the last session of Vatican II the tabling of a draft document that condemned Communism outright. His own expanded travels to far corners of the world, still novel when he took office, made them seem natural for John Paul II. His encyclical letter on the *Development of Peoples* deepened the Church's commitment to and involvement in the Third World, where the leadership of the Church is now expected in the popular efforts to win freedoms from repressive regimes.

The range and subtlety of Paul's use of the pastoral art could be observed when, within a few months of issuing a fairly traditional statement on women's role in Catholic services, he set up an international commission to study the needs and place of women in the Church, shortly thereafter receiving in an audience feminist leader Betty Friedan. "We wish to thank you," he said, "and congratulate you on your work." Like a man drawing music out of unlikely sources, Paul struck always that delicate balance between self-satisfied traditionalism and surprising innovation. Perhaps his artfulness is best observed in his way of dealing with the Vatican Museum. In the postconciliar popular uproar about the Vatican's hoarding such valuable art—could not this be sold and the money given to the poor?—Paul's response was classic. The Church protected art and the artist, he insisted, as he ordered that a new suite of galleries, devoted to modern art, be attached to the museum so that they abutted the Sistine Chapel itself. As he opened this addition he spoke of the Church's recognition—read, *his* recognition—that the artist's voice should be heard in the heart of the Vatican itself, that the Church was striving to hear, through the artist, what the world had to say.

What Paul accomplished was not merely a change in style but a shift in the distribution of practical political power within the once thoroughly *Roman* Catholic Church. He prepared the Church for change, for a greatly changed way of life that would allow, for example, the election of Karol Wojtyla, the first non-Italian Pope in centuries. Paul had set the stage for a new set of nonregal symbols for a Church that no longer modeled itself totally on the Roman Empire. The effects of his persistent modification of intra-Church symbols will continue, as he had shrewdly anticipated, long after more dramatic changes might have failed and been forgotten.

But such time-release gestures were not enough to please a world that received, with disbelief and skepticism, Paul's affirmation of the Church's ban on artificial methods of birth control. Not only did he dash the hopes for a change that he had raised by appointing a commission to investigate the matter but he disillusioned others who found the document disappointing in its theological substance and argumentation. His problem, of course, was that he did not believe that he could break the continuity of such a long-held teaching without damaging the Church in its own eyes and in the eyes of those who looked to it for consistency, and who had made difficult sacrifices to live by its teachings.

The publication of *Humanae Vitae,* however, marked a break in the willingness of millions of Catholics to accept the teaching authority of the Church. It was a moment of truth for many who felt that dogged insistence on a teaching that seemed so uncomprehending of the way people actually lived reflected an ecclesiastical mentality to which they could no longer submit. So many people by the millions began to trust their own judgment more than that of their Church. And they discovered that a large percentage of their pastors and confessors stood with them.

Other ecclesiastical observers note that Paul displayed strength and conviction in restating the Church's traditional position on birth control, since he knew that it was not what the world wanted to hear and that it would generate controversy. They suggest that this is also a classic example of Paul's use of the pastoral art. He was faced with the responsibility for keeping the Church together and for maintaining its unity of teaching and tradition. He could not easily repudiate his predecessors' teaching without opening other questions about ecclesiastical teaching authority that might have caused even greater dissension. But, even as the document was promulgated, he knew that he was initiating a period of intense theological study and dialogue on a sensitive issue. With his own hand Paul removed the words *definitivo judicio* from a draft of the encyclical and never pressed the document as an example of infallible teaching.

The discussion and debate that followed *Humanae Vitae* have innervated contradictory developments: massive and orderly dissent about birth control and other questions connected with human sexuality within the Church, while its leaders have ever more sharply upheld the ban on artificial contraception, finding in that issue a source and expression of their unity that they had seldom found so dramatically before. In other words, the issuance of *Humanae Vitae* achieved two goals that do not seem immediately compatible: increased theological dissent and increased unity among the Pope and the bishops. Two elements essential to a strong institution have thus been invigorated at the same time.

That outcome has, of course, not been applauded or, for that matter, understood by most participants in the discussions that followed *Humanae Vitae*. Indeed, the fact that the Pope permitted theological discussion of the issue during his lifetime represented an advance over the practice in previous ages in the Church. Still, in the judgment of many, this seems too small a gain to counterbalance the losses that the Church has suffered since the Pope spoke.

Critics point to the fact that adherence to the teachings of *Humanae Vitae* became a requirement for promotion to or within the ranks of the world's episcopate. No individual bishop has voiced any marked dissent, although some episcopal conferences, gaining a measure of strength and boldness from the anonymity of corporate statements, have raised the question of reexamining the Church's position. From the viewpoint of organizational solidarity, the encyclical has become a rallying point for administrators, and that probably has strengthened the Church as an institution. Never has the Pope's position been more central in the practical administration of the Church. Rarely, if ever, has so much pastoral concern for people been demonstrated on the plane of priestly ministry than in the understanding and support that have been extended on the everyday level of Church life. To have extracted a universal, if uncomfortable, allegiance from the world's bishops was no small achievement; it is that kind of loyalty which enables the institutional Church to weather the storms of history. Despite the dissent, the lowering of regard for authority, the disillusionment and suffering on all sides, the Catholic Church, as contorted by the process as the Elephant Man, still manages to make room for all those who, while fiercely debating this issue, identify themselves as Catholics.

Paul VI, it must also be remembered, committed himself to a conciliar Church and initiated regular synodal meetings of the world's bishops. Here again one observes his paradoxical approach to managing the Church's passage into the future. Realizing that the Church's monarchical model was spent of its usefulness, and convinced of the need for more practical collegial participation by the bishops in Church administration, he nevertheless maintained tight control over the agenda of those synods of which he was the president. He did not permit those gatherings to discuss priestly celibacy or birth control and, keenly aware that he was the Pope, he was quick to inform the day's presiding officer if he was displeased with the manner in which the debate had proceeded.

Following this style of forcing a dialectic between old and new, Paul expanded collegiality while insisting on the primacy of his own authority. Thus Leo Cardinal Suenens, who had stood on the balcony of St. Peter's with Paul immediately after his election, was summoned by the Pope during the coffee break that followed Suenens' synodal talk on ordaining women to the priesthood. The Belgian cardinal is reported to have said that Paul's quick confrontation with him not only ended the discussion but turned the day into "the worst" of his life. It is clear that Paul put his highest priority on preserving the Church's structural unity around the figure of a Pope with real power to undergird his symbolic grandeur. Collegiality could not be vital without some tension between the Pope and the bishops.

In time, Paul's vision of what the Church needs for survival may be understood and even acclaimed. It may prove to be as wise, for example, as his determination, against massive curial opposition, to appoint native bishops throughout the continent of Africa. It was too soon, he was told by advisers; the Africans were not prepared for such obligations. Sure of his judgment, Paul proceeded, and now, when African nationalism is a many-boroughed reality, the very ecclesiastics who fought the Pope on the issue take pride in the black African hierarchy that is fully in place.

Of such gambles with history, of such risks with the basic elements of ecclesiastical structures, did Paul, the seemingly distant Pope, fashion his papacy, always mixing the progressive with the traditional, incorporating the new but never at the expense of throwing away everything that was old. His judgment was that only a Church that survived precisely as a human institution could provide the setting for the mystical reality of its teaching.

Pope Paul VI may attract our attention now because, even to those who disagreed with his strategies, it was clear that he lived for the Church and for its survival rather than his own. In its cause, he allowed his own personality to recede. He did not cling to the papacy but emptied himself until, failing in health, he seemed almost translucent as he made his last journey to Castel Gandolfo. He may yet be recognized as the most remarkable churchman of the century.

John Paul I

JOHN PAUL I has already been wreathed in fables that do little service to his month-long pontificate. Variously embroidered versions of his death abound, in one of which the dossier of Chicago's Cardinal Cody lay spread across his coverlet; in the other version he clutches the *Imitation of Christ.* The central symbolic act of his few days rests in neither of these fantasies but in something he did, with humble sweetness, in view of the entire world. He acted with healthy instincts to reject a coronation and to banish the monarchical tiara from papal ceremonies. What Paul VI did only symbolically, by giving away one of his tiaras, John Paul did in fact and forever. He first chose the matchlessly symbolic combination of names to reveal his commitment to continued renewal. Then he elected to receive a woolen pallium as a symbol of pastoral service rather than the triple crown of the concluded regal era. As an image televised worldwide it remains far more valuable than a thousand theological arguments. John Paul I emotionally closed the monarchical era of the papacy by expressing his pastoral intuition through a ceremony that was to be followed by his successors. The one thing he was called to do, John Paul I did with extraordinary grace.

John Paul II

NOT SINCE Franklin D. Roosevelt and Winston Churchill has a public figure more quickly engaged the international imagination. And yet, although his face has become extraordinarily familiar, Pope John Paul II is also curiously unknown, both as an individual and as the maker of policy for the Catholic Church over the next generation. He has emerged pre-eminently as a man of paradox and contradiction. Someone new from a tradition that is very old, he is a spiritual leader for the West with roots in the East, a man by turns smiling and solemn. An unparalleled master of the electronic and print media, a pragmatic man living in and with the flow of contemporary events, he has become the first truly modern Pope. And yet he is fundamentally traditional and theologically conservative, a man who has been remarkably restrained so far in his administrative moves within the Church and startlingly bold in his dicey game of confrontation with Communism. To which century does he really belong?

He has eschewed the imperial trappings of papal authority and endeavored to make himself accessible, and yet some have criticized him for being out of touch with the reality and problems of priestly life today. He is a bona fide intellectual and an accomplished scholar, yet the Pope has disappointed many in some of his theological pronouncements because they seem to lack the richness and spiritual resonance expected of him. He appears theoretically willing to share ecclesiastical authority with his fellow bishops, but some Church observers fear that Pope John Paul II, cannily projecting his strong personality and accepting little advice from others, has emerged as a "super-bishop" who has treated his brothers in the episcopacy not as collegial partners but as legates who must continually prove their loyalty to him and his program.

A vigorous, healthy man who seems fully recovered from the grave wounds he received in the 1981 assassination attempt, John Paul may well oversee the passage of the Catholic Church into the next century. But what character will he finally impose on this oldest of institutions? Will this consummate actor get so caught up in performing that he fails to lead? Will he, in the end, become a personality rather than an authority with most Catholics? How, finally, will we come to know this man?

The election of Pope John Paul II, the first non-Italian Pope in nearly five hundred years, would not have been possible if enormous changes had not already taken place in the Catholic Church. The internationalization of the college of cardinals by Pope Paul VI made this body of papal electors more representative of the growing Catholic presence in the Third World, while it diminished the power of the Italian cardinals who, divided against each other in a bitter standoff at the conclave, made the election of a non-Italian possible. The Catholic

Church, whose character even in the Americas has so strongly reflected Western European traditions, is shifting its center of gravity rapidly. Demographers estimate that by the year 2000 the largest grouping of Catholics will be in the continent of Africa and, after that, in Latin America. Although the reality of this transformation has already been documented, its implications have hardly been imagined even in the Vatican itself, for it signals the coming end of Western dominance, the elision of *Roman* from the Roman Catholic Church.

When John Paul I refused the traditional symbols of the monarchical papacy, Europe's last eagle had fallen. When John Paul II confirmed these moves after his election and casually shattered the other traditions of regal remove by mingling with visitors and journalists, he acknowledged, perhaps unconsciously, that the identification of the Pope with crowned heads had been finally and irrevocably ended.

In fact the Pope's confidence and ease as a modern leader have already exasperated many aides who were more comfortable with popes who accepted the limitations and isolation of the Vatican's splendid misery. He refuses to eat alone, regularly has working lunches and dinners, and makes pastoral visits around the diocese of Rome, of which he is the bishop.

But the man who walked out of the Cold War into the contemporary world is also a fundamentally traditional and theologically conservative person. He could not have been elected had it not been clear to the cardinals in the conclave that he would carry out the platform of stabilized progress that they had agreed on before they were sealed into the Sistine Chapel to do their balloting. Pope John Paul's early moves to slow down, if not stop altogether, further modernization of Church policy in the area of human sexuality, priestly celibacy, birth control, marriage and divorce and abortion offered clear evidence of both his personal convictions and his readiness to carry out the mandate of the cardinals who chose him. Wojtyla was chosen, not because he was perceived as a man of his time, but because he was recognized as one committed strongly to a tradition that transcended time.

The new Pope's background has made him what he is, as sure a product of Polish Catholicism as O'Connell and Dearden were of different epochs of American Catholicism. He has lived his entire life in a country in which freedom has been the outcome of struggle rather than the gift of law. The Catholic Church has remained strong there, in the judgment of many, largely because it has never changed its traditions and practices. The bishops of Poland, dominated during the postwar period by the implacable Stefan Cardinal Wyszynski, archbishop of Warsaw, have kept a tight rein on the development of the reforms of the Second Vatican Council. The Church has remained the vigorous, clerically dominated phalanx of devout believers that it was before the council raised the vision of a new Church in which authority would be more widely shared by bishops and people. The Polish Church resembles the American Catholic Church of two generations ago: the churches are filled, the people are obedient and generous, and, because of their solidity and numbers, they constitute a force that must be reckoned with by the government. The faith has been central in their struggle with the Communist state.

Thoroughly Polish in his cultural and ecclesiastical experience, John Paul II found in his transition to the leadership of the Church of Rome a kind of "culture shock." He was not prepared to appreciate or understand the advanced thinking of the Church in Western countries on a wide variety of doctrinal and moral issues, even though Poland has quietly faced its own moral crisis. His conservative sensibility, masked by his public ebullience, was deeply challenged by firsthand contact with the realities of Catholic practice in Western Europe and North America. Many believe that he feels the Western democracies have been seduced by affluence and consumerism, which he has criticized as an evil that is the twin of socialist excess. Part of his call, he firmly believes, is to lead a crusade for firmer doctrine and discipline in the ranks of Catholics.

The first sign noted by Church insiders was Pope John Paul II's refusal to sign the dispensations from the priesthood that were on his desk when he assumed office. Apparently stunned by the Church's continuing acceptance of the fact that thousands of men had decided to resign from the priesthood, the Pope said that he could not in his heart give his approval. He has, for all practical purposes, halted the process. The matter is considered profoundly symbolic because it ties together the fabric of the priesthood, the issue of celibacy, and the possibilities of doctrinal development and disciplinary modifications. In his first Easter as Pope, John Paul issued a message to the priests of the world calling them back to an idealized, almost chivalrous vision of their vocation. It was a message that conveyed unmistakably John Paul's unequivocal commitment to clerical celibacy as an almost mystical element in the Church's life. He has reinforced this many times during his years on the throne of Peter.

Moreover, he has spoken of the traditional Church teaching on marriage, employing themes of sacrifice and interpretations of human love which, while noble and exhilarating, seem far removed, in the judgment of many, from the everyday experience of marriage by even the most zealous Christians. He has also directed remarks to religious women that reveal no acquaintanceship with their modernization and their aspiration to a greater participation in ministry, including the possibility of becoming priests. He has almost condescendingly urged traditional values on them, including the resumption of distinctive religious habits.

It may be natural for the Pope to judge that what has apparently been so hugely successful for Poland's Catholicism will also be good for the Catholicism of the world at large. Many Church leaders, however, are troubled by this attitude, which for a man as intelligent and as sophisticated as the Pope is remarkably without nuance. Perhaps the most widespread appraisal of John Paul is that he has previously unsuspected dimensions of personality. The world has come to know him as a theatrical man who thrives on working large public gatherings with the skill of a master actor or, what might be the same, a consummate politician who aims to alter the geopolitical balance of Europe.

The young Wojtyla trained for the theater in Poland and had extensive experience with a dramatic troupe there. His actor's instincts are obvious as he selects for attention a child from a large crowd or uses a finely calibrated sense of timing to solidify his rapport with an audience. The world has already grown familiar with the craggy, slightly hunch-shouldered Pope, his face in a Slavic half smile of restraint and expectation as he descends the airplane steps, his white shoulder cape rising in the wind and then falling over his head like a monk's cowl as he kisses the earth. It is a superb performance on one level, even if it is the heartfelt gesture of a deeply moved pilgrim on the other. Indeed, the Pope is a visual image of extraordinary grace and force, but few can remember what he has said on any occasion, and there are some who are beginning to examine his texts more critically.

His words have often been homilies encouraging com-
municants to highly stylized devotions, and many feel
that this is not the same as articulating a spirituality for a
hungry world. His first encyclical, *Redemptor Hominis,*
reportedly written by himself in longhand, proved to be
less the call to a fuller spiritual sense than many expected
from a man coming from the same tradition as Aleksandr
Solzhenitsyn. Some critics say that the Pope's considerable energy is so consumed by audiences, pastoral visits
in Rome, and travels abroad that he has not been able to
give his full attention to planning projects and routine
Church administration.

It is clear, however, that he is quite comfortable as the
Vicar of Christ, that he does not seem intimidated by
Vatican life or his entourage, and that in his day-to-day
dealings with others he continues to project competence
and warmth. In business dealings, however, John Paul
often displays a reserve that contrasts sharply with his
public persona. More than one ecclesiastical leader has
commented on his studied emotional restraint and on his
manner of seldom looking directly at a visitor. In interviews he employs a questioning style that does not reveal
the thread of his inquiry. He also avoids eye contact by
scanning the walls and ceiling of his office. Many ac-
quaintances believe that John Paul has always been an
outwardly gregarious but enormously self-contained
person and that, while he has inspired loyalty among
subordinates and affection in crowds, he does not have
intimate personal friends. He would not be the first great
man so described; indeed, such reserve may be characteristic of supremely gifted leaders who often believe in
hiding something about themselves, in preserving the
mystery that Charles de Gaulle considered an essential
quality of majestic leadership.

John Paul has also shown a sure capacity to stage and

use events, especially those widely covered by the media, to increase his own strength. Thus, as cardinal archbishop of Cracow, he received many American Church leaders on their visits to Poland, treating them with great respect and hospitality, while admitting that their presence was of great use to him in proving to the Polish government that the Catholic Church had highly placed friends in the West. He also knows how to use humor to defuse a tense or otherwise uncomfortable situation and he frequently employs ironic observations for that purpose. Cutting his wine with water at a dinner with American bishops shortly before his election, he listened without comment as they severely criticized the Swiss theologian, Hans Küng. Finally, with his actor's timing, he asked about whom they were talking: Was this John Krol, the cardinal of Philadelphia, they were discussing? (John Krol and Hans Küng are the same name, John King, in translation.)

John Paul has also always made it clear that he is the sole possessor of authority in any position in which he has served. He complained promptly, for example, when an abbot from a religious order near Cracow was reported to have worn his miter, the symbol of his rule, outside the monastery of his jurisdiction. That quick assertion of the prerogatives of one's position may be the prime characteristic of leaders who remain in power for long periods of time: there is never an obvious number two man in their retinue.

The Pope's virile and imposing presence, his self-control and self-confidence, his very strength have troubled many bishops, who feel that a theological issue of the highest order is the Pope's relationship to the Church's bishops. The doctrine of collegiality that was discussed at Vatican Council II says that the Pope does not dole out part of his supreme ecclesiastical authority to his brother bishops but that they possess authority on their own, by virtue of their episcopal ordination, which stands apart from, but is to be exercised in collaboration with, the bishop of Rome. This principle has been given concrete expression in the synods of bishops which, although held regularly during the last fifteen years, have been consultative in their deliberations.

As archbishop of Cracow, Wojtyla participated in these biennial convocations, and he is, therefore, well acquainted with the principle of collegiality. Many point to his action in allowing the bishops who assembled several years ago in Puebla, Mexico, for a special conference on the Church's role in social action in the Third World to make their own decisions and draw up their own final statement, not a word of which would be changed when it was submitted to him. He made every effort to control the agenda of the synod held in the fall of 1983, emphasizing the need for a return to individual confession as the desired outcome of the deliberations. Many delegates resisted this, seeing the question of penance and reconciliation as more complex than the Pope. There was no doubt, however, of John Paul's position or of his convictions about the need to return to styles of devotion that dated to the time of his upbringing.

In the same season, the Pope used the occasion of *ad limina* visits, especially by American bishops, to lecture them, almost as if they were schoolboys, about allegedly flabby Western spirituality. He suggested that bishops would prove their loyalty to Rome by withdrawing support from persons who even spoke out in favor of the ordination of women. His insistence that denying women an opportunity for dialogue on this major issue was not prejudicial to their human rights was judged by many to betray a lack of theological sophistication as well as an insensitivity to the evolution of equality for women as one of the major themes of twentieth-century history. The American bishops, in a series of interviews, put as good a face on these developments as possible, insisting that they welcomed the Pope's active interest in their work. Behind the scenes, however, Church leaders expressed amazement at the Pope's tightly focused agenda and the intensity of his commitment to goals which he has chosen almost entirely on his own. His refusal of counsel and the pace of his activity caused the President of an American Catholic university to wonder if John Paul had a sense of time's running out swiftly.

The Pope further increased the tension between himself and the American hierarchy by authorizing visitations of bishops about whom he had apparently received certain complaints. These included Archbishop Raymond Hunthousen of Seattle, a leading opponent of nuclear arms, and Bishop Walter Francis Sullivan of Richmond, Virginia. These were openly described as "investigations" and have few parallels in recent Church history. That they occurred offers further proof of the Pope's suspicions about the alleged "decadence" of American Catholicism. While many American bishops noted John Paul's willingness to listen to their defense of American Catholics, there is little practical evidence that he experiences anything but skepticism about their faith life.

These developments have underscored doubts as to whether John Paul will allow churches in other countries to grow according to their own traditions under the leadership of their own bishops or whether he may increasingly urge their return to a model of Catholic life that has passed away and that, even in his native Poland, is not as vigorous or successful as he supposes.

Leading theologians remain concerned because the

Pope speaks on certain issues, such as women's right to ordination, without an apparent deep understanding or a sure grounding in current theology. He has demonstrated in his writings that he is an accomplished scholar. Indeed, his philosophical work, "The Acting Person," is richly human and personalistic in content. There has, however, been little crossover from this to his theology, which is far more traditional and, in the judgment of many, dated. There is little evidence that John Paul, who has so dramatically encouraged freedom in Poland, encourages it among theologians.

Central to any of these issues is the question of just how much practical authority the Pope retains in a vastly changed world. While papal authority over the lives of Catholics was once almost total and uncontested, as it was during the reign of Pope Pius XII, the capacity of the Pope to command moral obedience, or even to attract favorable attention to his teachings, has eroded profoundly in recent years. When Catholics follow their own consciences about the intimate decisions of their lives, a Pope may destroy his authority by insisting upon it when many people do not feel guilty for ignoring it. As Richard McBrien, chairman of the Department of Theology at the University of Notre Dame, has said, the Pope has become a personality rather than an authority for Catholics. If Stalin once mocked the Pope by asking how many divisions he had, others may now ask how quickly these divisions will respond if the Pope summons them to battle.

Many also point to the fact that, although John Paul is comfortable in several languages, he has been intimately associated only with the Polish experience, something with which he has identified more intimately as the years have passed. Indeed, some suspect that his intense concern on Poland has distorted his views of everything else.

Thus he may accept the oversimplified interpretations of Catholic life in Western countries painted by some Vatican officials: that the West has declined spiritually and that the problems of the Catholic Church in places like the United States can be traced to a loss of faith that reflects a trend toward moral relativism and a lack of respect for authority. The Pope, according to a leading American churchman, rates the Church in the United States at least a notch or two below that in many other countries.

Poland, however, despite the surface manifestations of buoyant faith, is far from idyllic. National pride is extremely important, but one official in the Pope's old diocese of Cracow admits, "Don't believe that the West is alone in struggling with serious moral problems. We have exactly the same difficulties." This is underscored by the fact that half the pregnancies in a country that is ninety-five percent Catholic are terminated by abortion. In 1976 almost 400,000 abortions were performed in a country whose population is about 35 million, a proportion higher than that of the United States that year. The proportion of priests to people is higher in the United States than in Poland. While the Pope may be no stranger to the problems of the supposedly dying Catholicism of the West, he may come from a hierarchy that has not discussed such issues with the openness characteristic of the West.

The college of cardinals, now filled with black, brown, and yellow faces from faraway countries, symbolizes the emergence of the Third World as a force within the Church. Not only is the bulk of the Catholic population shifting into these areas but Latin American theologians have strongly advocated that the Church not only fight for its own life but also place itself in the forefront of the battle for social justice. Although no one can predict the ramifications of such changes, advanced theological thought, such as that expressed by the enormously influential German Jesuit Karl Rahner, foresees a world in which the Roman cultural dominance of the Church will sharply diminish. In each country the Church may well have its own language, its own traditions based on national experience, and a morality born of local realities rather than one exported from Roman officialdom.

This would require active decentralization and the practical embrace of the principle of collegiality. While de-Romanizing the Church would necessarily follow, so too would remarkably broad opportunities for ecumenical cooperation. Pope John Paul has strongly emphasized ecumenism but whether he can realize it while tightening up life within the Catholic Church remains to be seen. The dynamics of these changes are already engaged and there is no effective way to stop them or to turn back to the calm and well-ordered religious life that so many remember fondly. In other words, history may be running ahead of the Pope who has inserted himself so profoundly into its flow.

After more than five years in office, John Paul's aims are quite clear. He may, in fact, be so absorbed in and by the attainment of his objectives that he can no longer observe himself with any distance or sense of proportion. He belongs to two epochs of the Church, for he is at once the most modern and the most paternalistic and authoritarian of popes. His central preoccupation and commitment lie in one of the most daring episodes of modern history, the liberation of Poland. His heart and mind are wrapped up in this endeavor and he would willingly lay down his life or his papal crown—or at least make the highly dramatic gesture to do so—in order to achieve this. This powerful man's urgent pursuit of his destiny has begun to have psychological effects in other parts of the world. These include a lessening of his capacity to rule the Church of the West and a diminution of practically effective papal authority in the wider, non-Polish experience of Catholicism.

He has dedicated himself to a major political role, even as he forbids such activities to priests and nuns, and has made obvious his goal of achieving nothing less than victory in the Cold War in which he lived most of his priestly years. This exclusivity of emphasis allows Catholics in other lands to see him in a way that may free them rather than bind them to him. They respect him and honor him but they may not identify completely with his aims and they may not even cooperate with him in carrying them out. Such Catholics are liberating themselves from dependence on the papal authority he has used so prodigally in liberating his native land. They, at the same time, retain respect for the Pope and feel no need to rebel against papal authority that no longer binds them psychologically as tightly as it once did.

These Catholics are more confident of their own moral and religious judgments, they trust their own national traditions at least as much as the Pope trusts his. Emphasis on national Catholicism is catching. A major outcome —surely unforeseen by John Paul II—of his operational Polish Catholic nationalism will be an increased willingness for Catholics to distinguish his immediate historical goals from those of the universal Church. The Pope, single-eyed in his regard for Poland as the model Catholic country, may thereby actually create the environment in which the churches of the Third World, especially in Africa and Asia, can emerge with a better-defined identity of their own and a greater willingness to defend their own customs and traditions, for an indigenous Catholicism liberated fully from the Roman mind-set and from the conflicts, such as that over celibacy, that are the heritage of medieval European history.

The dynamic of John Paul's papacy will lead to the very outcomes he is attempting to forestall. He has not, for example, settled the role of women in the Church; he has, if anything, intensified its discussion and made educated people conclude that on such issues the Pope reflects his own life history far more than a commanding view from the throne of Peter. In an ironic reverse image of Paul VI's shrewd double-edged strategy, John Paul offers two messages in himself. By the very methods he employs to consolidate the life of the Church under the remembered banners of his youth, he dates both them and himself. He thereby makes it psychologically more easy respectfully to reject his views without rejecting him or the notion of the papacy. He is facilitating progress toward a greatly changed Church by so obviously defining himself as a product of an era that has come to a close. He has increased the tension essential to healthy collegiality, making the position of bishops more difficult, as they must speak up for themselves and their own traditions. That invigorates episcopal dialogue with the Pope and therefore strengthens the collegial model. John Paul is forcing this model to work more practically and more politically even though this may not be his main intention. Standing against history, John Paul accents its inexorable progress. This results in the reinforcement of the papal office not as one of splendid all-powerful isolation but as integrated into vital relationship with the world's bishops. John Paul may be preparing the kind of Church Karl Rahner has foreseen, hastening the very changes that he thinks he is slowing down. The goal for such a Church will be the restoration of the universal pastoral symbols that will give a living bond to an increasingly diverse Church.

PROSPECTS

PROSPECTS

Reading the Signs

THE immigrant Church of O'Connell, Spellman, Mundelein, and other doughty princes of a previous age has yielded to the measured collegiality of the Peace Church of Dearden and Bernardin. The essential characteristic of this new Church is its commitment to negotiation and to the dialogue which this demands. The obsessiveness of the present cohort of bishops serves them well in an age in which giving their attention to others, rather than issuing statements, is their principal means of displaying and exercising their authority. In the new American Church, personality, which in its grander episcopal manifestations, as with "Gangplank Bill," added flair to the older Church, is muted, subordinated at every turn to process. Collaboration and dialogue constitute the central and psychologically indispensable identifying mark of contemporary episcopal pastoral style.

Such collegiality in no way deflects bishops from the fundamental loyalty to Rome and to the preservation and enhancement of the Pope's position in relationship to them. Authority, however, is no longer incarnated in authoritarianism, for both theoretical and practical reasons. The theology of Vatican II restored the balance between Pope and bishops, binding it firmly to apostolic collaboration and providing the means, such as national episcopal conferences and synods, through which it could be put into practice. More important than this familiar theological justification is the bishops' pragmatic realization that authority expressed in any other way would not work. It is doubtful that any American bishops, no matter how democratic or popular, could exact obedience from their people on any issue, religious or secular, at the present time. While Cardinal O'Connell was known for endorsing candidates—he is given credit for inflicting a last hurrah on Boston's Mayor James Curley—and effectively marshaling the support of the Catholic electorate on a variety of referenda, it is presently unthinkable that an American bishop should even be tempted to try anything similar. The problem lies deeper than just staying away from politics, since, except in certain extremely safe areas, the bishops would lose their authority through the very act of exercising it. Catholic people accept their statements as *their* statements, as they are coming to accept the Pope's as *his* statements, but they do not feel compelled to obey them automatically.

Nor, it may be said, do the bishops expect them to do so. That is why everything, including the 1983 Peace Letter, is put in the context of continuing dialogue. Bishops prefer the people to study and discuss issues, exchanging opposing views and opinions, as they work toward broad statements that can bear the sometimes staggering weight of the combined input—until, in other words, a document reflective of all elements of the Catholic tradition is hammered out. The bishops' justly celebrated letter on "The Challenge of Peace," accepted by them at their May 1983 meeting, illustrates this process. That document went through three renderings, absorbing contributions and critiques from a wide range of Catholic and non-Catholic sources, and was studied in exhausting and exhaustive detail by the bishops themselves, who wanted to be as unified as possible in their approach to it. Behind this process stood the master of contemporary negotiation, Joseph Cardinal Bernardin, whose capacity to meet, listen, revise, and meet again— and begin again at first light—exemplifies the present pastoral style of the American bishops. That does not mean that they have abandoned their conviction that they possess authority handed down from the apostles. They know, however, that, except if it be processed collegially, such authority would truly be lost. It is this insistence on collaborative work that has drawn down on them severe criticism from those who prefer an older assertion of Church authority.

In a curious way, the present American bishops represent the high point of the authoritarian episcopal culture for which they profess now to have little taste and whose imperial style they have operationally disowned. Still, the current crop of bishops came out of the last great generations of the immigrant Church. Those in major leadership positions within the conference were born between the wars and experienced seminary training that owed its military style and anti-intellectual bias to the repressive Vatican actions at the very beginning of the century. These men are very bright and, as evidenced in the personal sacrifices most of them make in order to fulfill their obligations, they are profoundly dutiful and obsessive. Psychological studies carried out by Professor Frank Kobler at Loyola University of Chicago reveal them as personally strong, intelligent, but not creative men. They have no relish for ambiguity. Settling things through administration: this is their strong point and, despite demurrers, they take their greatest pleasure in discharging routine work. Process, in other words, is its own reward.

Gathered in May 1983 in assembly to review the hundreds of amendments that had been offered to their letter on peace, they resembled a large class of serious students, each of whom would stick to the wearying task at hand until it was completed. An institution that possesses such dogged and good-willed administrators enjoys enormous foundational strength. No quality—not piety, not prayerfulness—characterizes the American bishops better than doggedness in the fulfillment of the tasks that they feel they have been called by Providence to achieve. They are firmly committed to the episcopal myth that energizes their lives; their belief in it—and its central notion of their having been chosen from all eternity—is the root of their dedication to the Church and, if they do not feel weighed down, as most of them do not, or too puffed up, as few of them do, they function with great determination and clear consciences.

The core psychological strength of the self-perception of American bishops is their connection with the Roman authority through which they were "called" to their episcopal state. They were selected out of the hundreds if not thousands of young men who entered seminaries in and around them. They are the flower of the immigrant culture, and if they know that they have moved beyond it they also know that they arose from it. It is conceivable that as they gathered at Chicago for their spring 1983 meeting to vote almost unanimously for their pastoral letter on peace the American bishopric was at its best, that in this fulfillment of their dutiful pledges to the process of collegial discernment its members also fulfilled their own promise, justified the process that selected them, paid due honor to the parents and other forebears who gloried in their entrance to the priesthood and their accession to the episcopacy, that they bowed in the direction of the immigrant Church. Regarding them from a balcony seat, one felt that once they were dispersed they would never meet again in quite the same way.

Indeed, the bittersweet truth is that, because the Church from which they came exists no more, there is no rich source of supply from which to draw their own successors, that they symbolize not only the end of the immigrant Church but the end of their own special moment of leadership. The coming test is whether they realize that the changes in Catholic culture, which they had previously viewed from some distance, have now caught up with them. They must think about—or begin the process of talking about—a Church not only without priests but without bishops as well. At least they must entertain the thought of a Church that for the next century will necessarily possess a far stronger lay character than it ever has in the American experience.

This issue is obscured as the American bishops enjoy their point of highest esteem in American culture. As has been observed, these men constitute an impressive foundation for the postimmigrant American Church. The big question, however, is about the superstructure. Who will inhabit it or, for that matter, care about or for it? The immigrant Church built a huge physical plant, staffed by hundreds of thousands of people, including priests and religious men and women. The very institutionality of it guaranteed that it would enjoy the life that flows naturally from any busy gathering of human beings. The institution, after all, generated countless official communities, an array of departments and offices, even a multileveled Catholic press to report on all the activity. The immigrant Church talked to itself about itself a great deal. It resembled a large family that filled the house of its existence with a buzz of excitement. Something was always going on; anniversaries, professions, and ordinations were constantly being celebrated, Catholic football and basketball teams were always locked in combat, a hundred and more activities were generated every day by and specific to this bustling, highly centralized culture.

By its very size—just by the extent of its school system —by the fact that it seemed, under monarchical authority, to speak with one voice—the immigrant Church constituted an energetic and clearly identifiable presence within the larger culture. It was, in fact, this expansive structure that created the places—and the great spaces, physical, spiritual, and psychological—as well as the mildly elegiac mood that sustained an obsessive yet romantic epoch of American Catholic life.

In other words, the vigor of the immigrant Church in cities such as New York, Chicago, and Los Angeles was intrinsically related to its tight sociological structure, its intact obsessive defenses, its capacity to exist self-sufficiently within the host American culture. Movements flowed from it like the gushes from open hydrants; these were institutionally based and supported. To observe their intimate relationship to the root of the culture is not to count as less these activities—the thousand phenomena of Catholic existence—but to acknowledge that American Catholicism was enormously successful because it created such a rich and sturdy institutional base.

Now that the immigrant Church has come to an end, so too have many of its staples, from the Catholic press, to religious articles stores, to vocations, which depended on the stability of the culture of the Church. One of the structures of the old Church that survives, although in new form, is the conference of bishops, whose being is practically merged with that of the institutional Church, and an older generation of priests, religious, and lay people whose lives were previously deeply involved in the movements and activities of the same institutional Church. Examine the people who speak, write, or argue about what the bishops are doing, or how Catholics should be involved in any of a dozen noble causes, and you discover persons who, in large numbers, have always been invested in the institutional Church. They are not exaggerating when they say the Church is their home.

A failure to recognize this leads to a misrepresentation or a misreading of many of the late-century phenomena of American Catholic life. Even the bishops sometimes pit themselves against people who, although differing with them in some ways, are remarkably like them in others, that is, they are as committed to the Church as an institution as the bishops themselves. The famous Call to Action conference held in Detroit in the bicentennial year offers a clear example of this. While it was publicized as a confrontation between the bishops and Catholics, this was true only in superficial ways. Almost four fifths of the nonepiscopal participants were Catholics whose lives were centered in the institution, whose survival they wanted to promote as much as any bishop present. The assembly was constituted of bishops, priests, and men and women religious, who had grown up in the structures of the immigrant Church, who, in some ways, knew no other world. They may have differed on what will one day be regarded as superficial questions (e.g., celibacy and women priests) but they shared almost everything else in common. It was a family reunion, in a sense, and was a symbol of unity far more than of diversity in the American Catholic Church.

As these people have grown older most of them, even those who have resigned from the priesthood and religious life, have retained their interest and participation in Catholic causes. When Joseph Cardinal Bernardin addressed the priests of Chicago for the first time in August 1982, one of the most striking aspects of the gathering was the obvious graying of the clergy. The new archbishop was moving into a diocese in which middle age would be considered young for the members of the priesthood and religious communities. These servants remain, even in diminished numbers, in place and yet the clock is running on them as it is on the ranks of lay people who for generations have been so deeply involved in the Catholic culture and its many enterprises.

The unanswered, perhaps unasked, question wonders where the rest of the Catholic population is and whether members of its young adult generation perceive the Church, or aspire to any involvement with its institutional functions, in any manner like that which was commonplace within the last great generations to mature inside the immigrant enterprise. Young people now lead different lives and, even if they remain committed to the Church, the numbers who will become seriously involved in its institutional work will remain relatively small. The immigrant Church has passed into history and is gradually pulling after it a generation of exceptional bishops and that large, energetic family of activist Catholics who gave the Church its greatest era of institutional vigor.

Younger Catholics may be psychologically well prepared for a Church that allows its symbols to do a good deal of its talking for it. They have grown up in the space age. They will respond automatically to a Church whose worship offers them the opportunity to see deeply into the religious dimension of life. The present bishops, full of fond memories for the activist Church, may have to oversee something with which most of them are not very comfortable: a freer, more symbolic faith, one in which they must profess belief rather than manage or control. As a frame is to the work of an artist who speaks directly to the unconscious so must the bishop be to a faith that is best found in its symbolic riches, such as the Eucharist. Administrators, like framers, provide a setting that is meant to accent but never dominate—and certainly not literally explain—the essential mystery of the Catholic faith. The space age requires much more reliance on the profound religious symbols that speak to its inner reality than a reworking or redesign of the filigreed overlay of the authoritarian age.

The famous pantomimist, Marcel Marceau, explained in the early seventies that he had incorporated a routine to capture space exploration. Adults did not understand what he was up to at all but children, raised with a more direct consciousness of the age into which they had entered, appreciated it immediately. They did not need to have it explained to them. They "got" it because their own experience allowed them to resonate to the symbolic presentation. This is the same challenge with which the Church, on a dozen different levels, is dealing. It is much harder for adults to adjust to a religion more dominated by symbol than it will be for a generation at ease in the environment of space. Indeed, the successful passage of the Church into this new era demands that it open its treasure of symbols, new and old. It possesses extraordinary nonrational resources for the journey.

It is to the young, who cannot be satisfied with a retread of the authoritarian Church, to whom the wealth of the Church's unconscious must be thrown open. Even now young adults, returning to church after an absence sometimes of many years, speak of their response, not so much to sermons or to some elder's urging them to go, as to the mass itself. The Eucharist possesses an abiding power; it speaks in a language that cuts through time. The future of the Church depends on having more faith in its central mystery than in its rational administrative procedures. The latter exist only for the sake of the former.

The future of the American Catholic Church as a cohesive source of identity and influence on society may well depend on its leaders' ability to face a challenge that goes against the grain of their dutiful managerial instincts: to let go of the Church in a way, to let literal and authoritarian interpretations fade so that the heaped-up treasures of the Catholic tradition, the Church's only genuine wealth, can be approached and possessed in a new and mature way.

Pastoral Sense, Pastoral Church:
A Case History

ROMAN CATHOLIC administrative structures have always been inadequate housing for the Church's essential mystery. The language of symbols, which holds meaning as a watch holds time, is far better suited for a Church that, despite a long Roman connection, has never been summed up in one culture or one time period. Mysteries can never be reduced to rational sets of regulations. The Church proved that by successfully surviving what many considered its complete rational definition in the code of canon law. Too much law, as the struggles of contemporary society fully attest, cripples human communities. Dependence on law erodes the ordinary but indispensable mysteries of trust, honesty, and friendship. Settling everything through the law, as St. Paul once warned, should be a last resort rather than a first choice for believers. The Catholic Church has kept in touch through twenty centuries with the sacramental impulses of its own mysterious heart and has retained the capacity to speak lavishly of them in symbols that transcend the law, confound excessive rationality, but reach the human heart. That capacity, long restrained, is vital for its pilgrimage into the next century.

The Church has also maintained a sense about humanity's ways, a feeling for the events and passages through which men and women grasp true hints about the meaning of their identity and existence. The sacramental Church has always underscored and celebrated certain moments—those of love and suffering and death, of beginnings and endings, of separation and reunion—as *the* moments during which we sense our wholeness and our relatedness to each other. These are the occasions of mystery and meaning, the times in which we are religious, if we are ever to be religious at all. This is the pastoral, sacramental sense of the Catholic Church, its sometimes secret but perennial strength. Its pastoral feeling has outlasted its greatest worldly success, as well as its defeats, exile, and monarchy, and, of course, that code of canon law.

The ecclesiastical structure dominated by a sense of psychological obligation, staked like a vast tent, into position by authoritarianism, has collapsed and the emotional manipulation of guilt over religious duties is no longer pervasive or even possible. Over the last twenty years the American Catholic community has achieved increasing freedom and self-determination in resolving its moral conflicts. An exaggerated sense of personal guilt was buried in the wreckage of the immigrant Church. Interred at the same time was the central dynamic of control on which the practical authority of pastors and bishops had for so long rested. Blind obedience and unquestioning assent were dependent on the obsessive emotional mood of the old order remaining intact and in place. Associated phenomena included religious scrupulosity, regular confession, and an oversupply of applicants for seminaries and religious houses. Their decline is a sign of a mystery shaking itself free of the accretions and burdens of the monarchical age. Decreasing vocations, in this interpretation, do not constitute a problem but a solution to a problem that existed when the Church was so topheavy with vocations that its nature seemed essentially clerical and there was little room for genuine participation in the Church by laity. Having fewer priests by no means suggests that we do not have enough priests for a healthy future.

Now that the authoritarian age has passed, what binds the community of the Church effectively together? The Church, it has been suggested, is now freer to enjoy once again a response richly textured with mystery. The identifying style of the now and future Church is *pastoral,* which is comparable to that of a family that works out its challenges and troubles through its members' relationships with each other rather than through the application of absolute rules or through arbitration by a lawyer. The pastoral approach of the Church, human rather than legal, has always addressed itself to the tensions that arise between it and its members in regard to its teachings, traditions, and practices. The pastoral reality of the Church is its only effective *religious* incarnation in the lives of most people. It is the occasion for the sacramental ministry that defines the Church's only important business.

The pastoral relationship, which is marked by understanding and compassion, resolves the tension between the ideal of Church doctrine and the reality of everyday life by giving due attention to the principle of teaching or discipline involved and also to the human plight of the persons affected by it. Through the pastoral mode Church leaders are able validly to represent the teachings which they are committed to support while at the same time they respond with active and comforting concern for Catholics who find themselves, for whatever reason, in conflict with some aspect of that reaching. Perhaps the most visible current pastoral response of the Church may be found in its reaching out to divorced and remarried Catholics, acknowledging their problem while making room for them within the community of the Church, embracing rather than exiling them. The pastoral approach allows people to live in peace in a continuing relationship to a Church that understands them. It is the secret of the Church's survival, the wonderful truth of its understanding of sinfulness, fate, and death that is appreciated by those who call themselves conservatives as well as those who think of themselves as progressives. This pastoral position is the *essential* Catholic insight into life.

Even in the dark ages of authoritarianism, many priests and religious preserved the pastoral sense in individual cases, extending the Church beyond its tight legal boundaries through their compassionate ministries. Horror stories are rightly told about the severe judgments and the harsh treatments that were sometimes handed down by dour ecclesiastics—such as the shameful manner in which mixed-marriage ceremonies were carried out in the mean surroundings of rectories or outside the altar rail—but the Church stayed alive in the more generous spirit that could always be found within it. The pastoral sense has always been the heart and soul of the underground Church that existed long before the notion became trendy in the sixties. This pastoral feeling for people was nourished by men and women who understood that the gospel was meant to be healing and freeing rather than condemning and enslaving. This has always been the Church's greatest strength, even when its lawgivers did not fully understand it. Through the pastoral mode, the Church was wiser than it seemed to be, closer to its people, surer of its transmission of the spirit of Jesus.

The authority of bishops and priests—and of the Pope himself—now depend on a pastoral rather than the executive style. As observed, any effort to exact obedience from believers by the Church under the threat of authoritarian punishment would now meet certain failure. The bishops can do anything with their authority but exercise it, immigrant Church fashion. That does not mean that the structure of the Church has collapsed and that we wander in ecclesiastical anarchy. As with vocations, the collapse is the solution rather than the problem. The world's bishops now must exercise their authority in a totally new way—like the apostles at Pentecost, they must speak in "entirely new languages"—through their pastoral relationships with their flocks rather than through legalistic edicts and pronouncements. This actually enhances their authority because it forces them into genuine leadership roles. The Catholic bishops, perhaps ahead of the administrators of many other world institutions, have successfully addressed the main problem of the last half of the twentieth century, that of reestablishing relational authority as a healthy and necessary aspect of life. While they may not have set out consciously to do so, and may not understand that they have done so, they have, better than most organizational leaders, achieved some measure of success in this regard. The collegial style is the medium through which a cooperative pastoral style has been refurbished, legitimated, and established as the way of doing business in the American Catholic Church. This supports authority whose vigor flows from pastoral understanding rather than imperial-style edicts.

The genius of the pastoral style represents not moral relativism or indifference but an active means through which the teachings of the Church, refined by current theological and scriptural scholarship, are applied to the realities of modern life. The bishops' pastoral letter on "The Challenge of Peace" offers the most prominent example of this approach. Through the process—essential to Catholic pastoral vision—of extensive consultation the American Catholic community was asked by its bishops to reflect on the implications of their religious teachings and traditions for the issue of nuclear war. This letter was not a directive from above; its strength lay in its grass-roots nature, in its development by bishops who were willing to modify and enlarge their convictions on the basis of their listening to the sense of the broader Christian community. The tentative, questioning style of the document, the extensive debates and discussions of its theological and scriptural grounding, as well as its ability to reflect the spectrum of the Catholic community's experience: these, operationally, define the pastoral process that will dominate the American Church over the next generation.

This approach keeps the Catholic community in relationship to its bishops and to the larger structures of Catholicity, not out of fear but out of faith, out of a newly fashioned loyalty to and respect for a process which creates a bond while it explores an issue. It also focuses on something bigger than the Church itself. Although American bishops may have adopted this strategy out of a dutiful compliance to the directives of Vatican II, it has also permitted them to follow the pastoral instincts that most of them feel despite their constitutional obsessiveness. The pastoral style is based on a vision of the Church as a teaching institution that appreciates the fact that it never stops learning about the mysteries which it proclaims. Rooted in an acknowledgment of the imperfection of human beings, such a pastoral approach makes no place for insistent demands for an unreal and impossible perfectionism. It has no need to create a world of its own. Such a Church institutionalizes a process through which continuing lay contributions to its thought and practice can be made systematically and effectively. Through the pastoral mode the American Church can prepare itself somewhat calmly for what otherwise would be contemplated as the tragedy of a priestless future. The avenue to the incorporation of the laity more vigorously and more responsibly into the Church is already open. This development is a function of a church that is not a brittle structure of laws, but rather a supple, responsive human organism guided by the Spirit.

This pastoral era is marked by dialogue rather than confrontation between the people and their Church leaders. The bishops are moderators and leaders of the dialogue rather than champions of one cause or another. Divisions of opinion obviously exist within contemporary American Catholicism, as, for example, in the spirited discussions that accompanied the development of the bishops' letter on nuclear arms. Still, even "progressives" and "conservatives" stand on more common ground than even they sometimes suppose. Howsoever poorly named—and one must always remember that the spokesmen for such groups represent a small fraction of the fifty million American Catholics—these "progressives" and "conservatives" are profoundly loyal to the Church and support its institutional features and its episcopal leadership. Their values—for life and for peace, among others—often overlap and their keenest arguments, such as those on biblical research, presuppose a commonality of faith and commitment to the gospel. They are drawing closer together, more tolerant of each other's views, as they reflect the pastoral style in a family way of disagreeing. Neither group, however, is trying to oust the other or prove, once and for all, that one is completely right and the other totally wrong. In times of difficulty they draw from the same sacramental core of the Church for their strength and consolation. They meet in the eucharistic mystery whether they always understand it or not.

*   *   *

A strain of profound expectation runs through the American Catholic consciousness. Catholics are always looking beyond the wintry present, past false starts and toward a rich, fragrant, and lasting spring. It isn't just heaven that they confidently anticipate, but better times in general, a triumph of the gospel in a world in which everything, including the Church itself, is made new.

This Christian optimism is far different from classic American positive thinking, that apple-cheeked Rotarian heartiness about the link between piety and prosperity. It is wisdom, as worn as old silver, about things of the spirit—a conviction, tested by desert wandering and made poignant by the echo of biblical lament, that the teachings of Jesus can still transform the world.

That powerful orientation to the future may cause people to miss the fact that a new Church has already come into being: a body of the faithful who identify themselves deeply with the mission of Catholicism. These faithful are, in fact, the Church that they hope for —a pastoral Church that, in and through them, is already in place.

People who are mature are not self-conscious about it. Perhaps that is why many Catholics have not noticed the growth they, as a Church, have achieved. A striking example of a more adult, varied new Church could be observed in a combination of incidents in Chicago, a diocese that was racked by dissension, strife, and uncertainty during the long unhappy twilight of the immigrant Church. Similar examples could be found in every diocese in the land. This one involved two tales of a city, and the pastoral passage out of the immigrant Church.

On Memorial Day, 1979, Walter Imbiorski died of a heart attack. He had been a prominent priest, a writer and lecturer of national reputation, who had married in early 1975. He continued to produce materials for Church projects until he died.

Chicago's archbishop, John Cardinal Cody, immediately advised the pastor of Imbiorski's parish that he could not hold services for the dead man because Roman authorities had never issued his official papers of laicization. What Christian farewell there might be for this extraordinary man would have to be confined to a stuffy funeral home on North Broadway.

Imbiorski had been well known and the cardinal's edict was widely reported in the Chicago newspapers; an NBC television crew showed up at the North Side funeral home where the wake was held. While his widow wept at the coffin, reporters sought sidewalk reactions to this denial of Christian burial to a former priest whose character seemed rich and pure in comparison with those of some of the hoodlums who, almost beyond counting over the years, had been granted funerals by the Church.

Cody did two things by forbidding Christian burial for Walter Imbiorski. He rattled the bones of a dead authoritarianism, thus raising a grotesque clatter which called the new Church together in a way that demonstrated how alive it was.

Hundreds of Catholics—priests, religious, and laity—forged a sign that rose from every part of the city—not to stage a protest against the cardinal's ruling but to do something grander by far: to carry out the simple Christian duty of burying the dead. These men and women came on their own, peacefully, undefiantly, certain of what they wanted to do: to keep vigil with and to comfort Imbiorski's widow, to become, in burying a son and brother, the Church itself.

Imbiorski's wake became an unplanned reunion for scores of people who had labored together in the causes with which Catholicism was identified—education, race relations, marriage preparation, liturgical progress, any and every pastoral service the Church had ever offered. It was a coming together of the rank and file who had taken the gospel seriously and who had applied its teachings in good times and in bad without surrendering to discouragement. They were not sorted out as progressives or conservatives. They gathered far more in joy than in anger, displaying the *sensus fidelium*, that trustworthy intuition of believing people which theologians have always identified as a sign of the real presence of the Church in life.

At the funeral home priests led prayers during the wake and again on the morning when Imbiorski's body, locked out of his parish church, was borne directly to the cemetery. These same people gathered again the next Monday night at the Basilica of the Queen of All Saints, invited by the pastor, Father Robert Clark, for a mass of resurrection for Walter Imbiorski.

More than a thousand people attended and mingled later at a reception in the school hall. The mood was peaceful rather than rebellious, the event having the special beauty of something that has finally been well and rightly done.

The people were—and knew well they were—the Church responding pastorally to death and loss. Through them, the Church—properly, lovingly, and unselfconsciously—buried one of its own. What chancery officials had denied him was accorded to Imbiorski by the living Church, a larger, more generous, more available community than that constituted by bureaucrats. The Church thought to be waiting in the future was found to be vigorously alive.

Three years later in the same archdiocese—which had been described as demoralized and divided during the long passion of Cardinal Cody's last months—believers gathered once again to welcome their new archbishop, Joseph L. Bernardin. Those who had buried Walter Imbiorski were among the throngs who joyfully celebrated the beginning of a new period in the history of one of the nation's largest archdioceses.

There was little talk of the late cardinal and the shadow of federal investigation that had fallen across his final anguished months. Nor was there evidence of dissension or bitterness between what have been styled conservative and liberal Catholics. Rather there was a spirit of readiness for the tasks ahead, an undeniable enthusiasm for the new work to be done on all the old issues. There was another unself-conscious manifestation that the Church of Chicago, as a new leader came to preside over it, was not sulking in exile, was not alienated or riven, but was alive to the faith and its challenges.

The remarkable truth beneath the deeply felt reception for Cardinal Bernardin is that of the maturity of the American Catholic Church. The reawakening of Chicago as a center of Catholic life is but one example of how deeply the faith has been sown into the soul of the believing community throughout the country.

Today, for American Catholics, the kingdom of God is indeed in the midst of them. Not perfect, but not sentimental or triumphant either, the Church that people have dreamed about for generations is an existential reality rather than a wispy vision. Its most distinguishing mark is that it has moved beyond the issues of authority and obedience which preoccupied and bedeviled both bishops and people for so long. Even if such a church's active membership is small, it still constitutes a remarkable and influential reality, remarkable leaven in the dough.

If Imbiorski was, in a sense, truly buried by the Church he served for so many years, it was accomplished by people who knew that, by their actions, they were neither challenging nor subverting the institutional Church. They were inspired by a deeper intuition about how a living church can group and regroup, can reach out and do the right thing whether there is official approval or not. That is the essence of the pastoral mode, the essence, indeed, of anything daring to call itself Catholic. The legalistic edict forbidding a Christian burial for Imbiorski did not prevent him from receiving one; neither did it give rise to a continuing bitter wrangle about whether it should have been done or not. A pastoral Church operates as an organic whole, incorporating and integrating its experiences, putting resolved conflicts behind it as it pursues its highest values.

The welcome of Cardinal Bernardin was heartfelt and genuine, not because the people felt that they needed an authority figure to supervise their lives, but because they wanted a pastor who would stand with his flock rather than define himself over and against it. The new archbishop arrived not to reassert the authority of his office but to invite the cooperation of his people in proclaiming the message of Jesus. The advent of Bernardin—bearer of the Dearden inheritance and typical of the generation of bishops now in leadership in the American Church— marks the close of a time when the Catholic community exhausted itself in debating the issues of authority and

obedience. The new Church represents the living resolution of that old problem through a common pastoral
vision of its mission to the world. The episcopal leaders of
this now and future Church have not only abandoned an
insistence on a lockstep response, they have gone far in
developing a pastoral sense of encouraging and supporting their flocks.

They have, for example, demonstrated remarkable
sensitivity in their ability to understand, absorb, and in-
tegrate much more about human sexuality than some
Roman documents would suggest. Not only have they
learned more about it, they have also institutionalized
these insights—as in their responses, built now into diocesan machinery, to divorced and remarried Catholics.
They have also shown a pastoral restraint in their discussion of contemporary Catholic attitudes toward birth
control. They have also defended their people to a questioning Pope. And they have drawn up a platform that,
in its focus on the great issues of nuclear arms, war and
peace, race and poverty, is a startling challenge to Catholics who want to apply their faith in the vast and needy
world that spreads beyond their private devotions.

This new Church is the direct product of the huge
American Catholic educational system, financed by the
sacrifices of immigrants and staffed by generations of
priests, religious, and dedicated lay persons. That today's
American Catholicism has vital, theologically sophisticated elements actively involved in defining and resolving contemporary ethical crises is a tribute to yesterday's
believers who made it all possible.

That is why it is dangerous to misread statistics and to
think that, because there are fewer priests and religious,
something has gone wrong in the American Church. The
shift in numbers, instead, signals that something has
been right with it. There may be fewer men and women

entering seminaries and convents but there are more men and women than ever with a sense of vocation about their responsibility for gospel values in their lives. There is, in other words, a leadership level of lay Catholics already in place. These American Catholics—among them, the hundreds who buried Walter Imbiorski and the hundreds of thousands who welcomed a new archbishop to Chicago—live with a commitment to serve their colleagues and their neighbors.

It would be sanguine to overestimate the absolute number of Catholics who stand ready to give of their time and energy in responsible ways to this new American Church. But there are more than enough to take on the tasks of ministry and education that are essential to the work of the institutional Church. Beyond them there are thousands more who, with a little encouragement, will carry their Catholic values deeper into the professional worlds of American society. The bishops are well prepared to use their pastoral style to harness this energy by widening the opportunities for responsible lay ministry in the ongoing future of the Church. This, in fact, is the obvious and essential task confronting the leaders of American Catholicism.

The Now and Future Church

AMERICA'S Catholic Church has watched its formerly ornate authoritarian scaffolding fall away like a booster rocket as it has climbed, along with all other human institutions, into the disorienting and horizonless space age. The Church is now challenged to maintain its institutional integrity while it continues to transform itself. Put in an oversimplified but useful way, the American Catholic Church, having jettisoned authoritarianism for good, must now reestablish itself as a model and font of healthy authority, not just to survive but to offer its best service to the world.

This movement out of dead authoritarianism into revitalized authority depends on the Church's capacity to understand the languages of symbol and myth, to translate and speak them comfortably rather than grudgingly so that it may preach a religion that speaks to the depths of the searching contemporary world. Institutional forms capable of restructuring themselves are essential to a faith that transcends literalism and proclaims a kingdom that is in the very midst of its people. Its authority arises, in this renewed moment, from its trustworthiness, from the sureness of its sacramental intuitions, from its capacity to catch the echoing cries of an anguished world and to respond with the bell-true resonation of the gospel of Jesus. The Church's future flows from the mid-century course correction of Vatican II which allowed it to surrender its stern demands for obedience and rediscover its gospel fidelity to humankind. People began listening to it as it renewed its pastoral commitment of service.

Obedience, in fact, derives from the root word "to listen to" and the healthy authority of a new Church depends on its ability to say something that people can and will listen to as it interprets their bewildering experience for them. Such a Church, which will necessarily look different from one culture to another, resembles persons who, without claiming authority, receive it as a gift from the listeners who recognize that they make sense. Authority in the space age is essentially a gift rather than a demand note payable to the bearer. Authority is possessed by those who interpret human experience in accurate and disinterested ways, motivated by a desire to understand rather than an urge to control. In recent history, for example, people stopped and listened when Pope John XXIII spoke or acted; he thereby did more to reestablish the papal right to address human affairs than a thousand closely reasoned theological arguments.

Jesus was listened to because he "spoke as one having authority." He compelled attention because he addressed himself accurately to the depths of human experience. People knew more about themselves and the direction they should follow from listening to him. Great poets and artists are recipients of authority because they

symbolize the experience of their times, making it possible for a searching society to understand itself. The
Church for this age must allow its powerful poetic side—
its prophetic side, to put it in more familiar terms—to be
revealed in and through modernized forms. Accurate
prophecy, rather than gabbled mystical prayer, is the
sign of a Church with authority.

Hardly an easy challenge and yet everywhere—in the
theology of Rahner, in the profound work of Campbell,
in the wisdom of the believing community itself—the
groundwork for a Church that changes through growth
has already been laid. Father Driscoll and his colleagues
at Dunwoodie saw this as the great task of the twentieth
century. What they began—and what seemed forgotten
with their abrupt dismissal from seminary education—
has survived as the enlightened basis for the Church of
pastoral collaboration. They were the unknown soldiers
in the "good cause," as Driscoll termed it, of reform.

This is not a romantic Church that operates mystically,
ideally, and impractically. Such a Church needs hardheaded and carefully developed structures as well as
leaders who are regarded as such and are invested with
effective operational symbols of authority. The transition
from the tiara to the woolen pallium as the instrument of
papal authority is an example of the kind of poetic institutional transformation that preserves continuity in a
new and more fitting form. The Church thus gives itself
up and finds itself in the same moment, discovering that
it is stronger and more authoritative as servant than as
master. Its vast organizational structure must continue
to transform itself to guarantee that it will be an adequate medium for the Church's pastoral ministry to the
human family. An institution—rather than a disem-
bodied, one-man-one-faith diaspora of eucharistic communities—must function in practical, down-to-earth, hu-

man fashion. Hardly beatific or free of tension, this Church perhaps multiplied in styles, lives vigorously in and through the ongoing collegial dialogue of its pastoral style. Authority purged of authoritarianism is its lofty, difficult, and absolutely necessary goal.

The Church of the interstellar age must have a discernible shape and be an agent of relationship to itself and its members as well as to those outside it. Such a Church can proclaim—with a new sensitivity to the depths of its content—a body of religious truths through its teaching and through its symbolic, liturgical life. As a visible organization it breathes in and out with the men and women and stands as a source of identification and meaning to those who seek communion with it. Its energies depend on a diversity of opinion; this allows for a vital presence as well as a shucking off, not only of vestiges of authoritarianism but also of the mindless substitutes for religion, such as shallow psychologizing, that have been taken on in recent years. A Church without a central nervous system innervating a complex structure soon disintegrates into the scattered sect mentality which Robert Bellah has so trenchantly criticized for its emphasis on privatism and the depoliticization of religious belief. A church is a public institution that reminds people of their common obligations, of a good greater than their self-interest. Such a church challenges a society by involving itself in the public issues in which religious truths are incarnated. The American bishops' involvement in the issue of nuclear arms, for which they have been criticized as meddlers in a question outside their ken, is the proof of their proclamation of mature and relevant faith.

Bellah, along with dozens of other social critics, has noted America's elevation of the individual and his or her own world to a dizzying centrality in life. A new authoritarianism resides in the unattached person, a tyranny is exercised by the person who counts on nobody, affiliates loyally with no one, and finds the beginning and end of gratification in the self. America, according to these observers, has been subtly remade into a nation of individualists who are unfamiliar with the discipline of self-sacrifice that is essential to the pursuit of the common good. Decisions are increasingly made on a self-referent basis with either a rejection of or a dulled perception of the possible effects of such choices on others. This leads to a muted ethical sense and enormous difficulties in areas which require trustworthy human communication. To such a society—more struggling for maturity than sinful—the American Church must relate itself, not as a controlling demagogue calling for repentance but as a fellow pilgrim whose authority arises from its own experience with all things human. Because the Church is well acquainted with sin and selfishness, it can help all those who struggle with these burdens.

One may only conclude that one of culture's most pressing needs is for a stable institution against which people can measure themselves, their conflicts, hopes, and aspirations.

Presently, the United States turns to the courts, especially the Supreme Court, rather than to the churches to resolve essential questions of meaning and morality. The fact that the decisions of the Supreme Court are thought to define the margins of constitutionality and of ethics illustrates the need for an insightful institution to reflect with pastoral concern on the morally open-ended problems that can never be settled satisfactorily by the courts.

Old-fashioned moralistic crusades do not, however, address themselves to the complex problems of a culture disenchanted with authority. Life without healthy authority is not a paradise but a vague purgatory in which no signpost can be trusted to give the right location or direction. Such a society must expend great energy and large sums of money in adjusting to the consequences of its lack of a reliable center of gravity. That is America's main problem as it scrambles to adjust, for example, to the breakdown of authority in the family by dealing with its multiple effects, that include the still uncharted long-term influences on children of divorce, separation, and serial marriages. Life by improvisation has yielded more rather than fewer problems over the last generation.

Instead of addressing the causes of the enormous problems people experience in establishing and maintaining truly satisfying relationships, we tend to tolerate and to some extent justify these patterns of unhappiness, to underwrite them, thus complicating them further. A society which accepts and, in effect, subsidizes the decline of the nuclear family may be doing the best it can to keep its balance in the space age. That, however, will not save it from the consequences of shattered relationships. Like it or not, there is abundant evidence to suggest that these result in people who have considerable difficulty with the basics of human relationships, with the fundamental experiences of faith, trust, and sacrificial love that stabilize and give life to friendship, marriage, the family, and, finally, the state itself. Even if it sticks just to the basics, the American Church clearly has enormous work ahead of it. When it speaks the gospel clearly, it meets such challenges very well. These impacted human difficulties are the wounds the Church is called to heal rather than condemn.

Almost without letting its left hand know what its right hand is doing, the Church of the mideighties is already preparing for a different look in the next century. The most prominent feature of the now and future Church is, of course, the collegiality that supports its pastoral style. This foundation is already in place and, given the present episcopal leadership of the American Church, will be the instrument of continuing pastoral reflection through which traditional teachings will be applied to societal problems. This will accentuate the debate between various wings of the Church while it also raises the intellectual level of the discussion. The achievement of this process consists in its openness to all sides, even to secular input and criticism, and its willingness to raise questions rather than to give final answers on significant issues. As such, it is a vehicle to stimulate the imagination of the concerned community of Catholic intellectuals who wish to have their voices heard in and through the Church. The American Church now possesses a forum for intelligent debate and discussion on the major issues of the day. The danger of sharp and destructive divisions is diminished when there is a process that encourages and mediates dialogue. The very commitment to this process of collegiality initiates a psychological experience that changes, to some extent, everyone who is connected with it.

One cannot involve oneself in a serious discussion without preparing well for it. This is far different from making generalizations based on limited human experience or forging bold statements out of personal prejudice. An opportunity for serious discussion with the aim of authoring a statement to which as many discussants as possible can agree automatically improves the climate of the exchange. Psychologically, it also allows persons to be heard who may find that even if their argument is modified through later discussion experience is in itself rewarding. Being heard was a novelty in the authoritarian Church. The process of collaborative discussion overcomes that old roadblock and also educates all those who participate in it. Persons of good will cannot fail to learn as they stretch their minds and imaginations to understand viewpoints other than their own. The postimmigrant Church thus has, as a central feature, a meeting place where mature exchanges of opinion can take place in a positive and constructive manner. This is an enormous advantage to a Church seriously committed to collegiality.

The subject matter of interest to the future American Church is as rich and broad as its attention to everything that admits of pastoral concern, to everything of human concern. That the bishops address themselves to war, economics, poverty, race, abortion, moral education, and a dozen other prominent problems defines the new Church's sense of values and stimulates the wider membership of the Church to take a role in shaping the discussions. The future Catholic community may resemble less an institution and more a movement based on gospel principles, one that works toward the change of the heart of society. It will, in a sense, be less churchy as it becomes more of a church.

Present assessments of the American Church in the popular media necessarily follow the instincts of those who report and comment on the news. The emphasis is on dramatic change interpreted as collapse, on the decline in the numbers of priests and religious, the close of seminaries, the apparent leveling off of church attendance. Reporters in general prefer to simplify and establish causation for a malaise. These causes, as in the Associated Press series Roman Catholicism that ran in the summer of 1983, are ordinarily assumed to be Vatican II and the 1968 encyclical *Humanae Vitae.* There is, however, another way to view the changes in American Catholicism that, without being romantic or naive, is hopeful and positive. The American Church is alive, dynamic, more at the center of its culture than it has ever been before.

The Church has, in fact, maintained its identity while it has weathered multiple changes rather well. The groups who hold differing opinions within it have not split off from each other; the tension of their debates is healthy for the Church. Vatican II, as has been observed, was hardly a cause but rather an event in a process of change that had been going on for many years. The council, in fact, allowed the Church to manage the necessary move from a monarchical to a more pastoral orientation to itself and the world. The encyclical *Humanae Vitae* encouraged more adult discussion, theological research, and serious examination of conscience than almost any document issued from any source during the sixties. It engendered not indifference but thought. That it prompted people to look within themselves to make moral decisions on intimate matters represents a step forward, away from priest-ridden sexual mores, away from dependence on authority for choices that men and women ultimately must conscientiously make for themselves.

Despite the problems and the pain of renewal—and they were no greater than the pain that came to people in different ways during the autocratic high noon of the immigrant Church—one cannot say that the Church is worse off now than it was before. The American Church, most importantly of all, now has a pastoral mechanism for processing the changes whose shapes have already risen on the horizon.

The Church in the United States, despite the media's focus and the Pope's skepticism about its faith, is already involved in preparing for the aspects of continuing change that are just beginning to work themselves out. It is not so much what people in the Church say, it is what they do that counts. Far-reaching changes have already been initiated on the level of behavior, the level that counts in the long run. An era of more prominence for the laity may be observed in the sketches and architects' drawings that are now being carefully prepared in various parts of the country. These plans are evolving with episcopal approval at a grass-roots level, with wide lay participation, using the elements of collegial discussion and negotiation that are the Dearden-Bernardin contribution to the American Catholic experience.

In the archdiocese of New York, for example, the chancery expects that only about half the 777 priests active in 1983 will be available for parish service in the year 2000. "We are a new church in a new world," said Monsignor Thomas Leonard, according to the New York *Times* (February 29, 1983). "We must find energy and take new initiatives because there is the same amount of work to be done." A discussion of the report on future priest supply was held, not at some underground church, but at the same St. Joseph's Seminary at which, eighty years before, Father James Driscoll had led his all too brief renaissance in Catholic theology and enlightened seminary training. The convocation was sponsored by Terence Cardinal Cooke, one of the most stable anchors of the American hierarchy, thus underscoring the meeting's significance and its predictive value. These administrative Church officials are not fighting a rearguard action against change but are preparing for a future which they expect to be radically different from the past. The Rev. Thomas Barrett, who compiled the report, was quoted as saying, "We simply must develop lay leadership better. In twenty or twenty-five years we're going to have an entirely different situation and it would be too late to do anything then. Either we do it now or it won't be done." These are not the words of men bitter that their world is changing but of priests sensitive to its inevitabilities who appreciate that it is the Church as a movement, not as a clerical culture, that must be preserved.

The New York priests, with their late archbishop's encouragement, looked to the revised code of canon law for the openings they needed to introduce laity in greater numbers at various levels of Church life. The new code allows lay people to preach in church, manage parish finances, and administer parish life as well as to serve as chancellors and to fill other functions once kept tightly in clerical hands. While these opportunities are not as broad as some would wish, they do represent a significant and approved breakthrough whose implications for the future are not difficult to appreciate. Similar plans and associated experiments are under way across the country, where the projections almost universally reveal a sharp drop in priests and religious before the year 2000.

In Indianapolis, Indiana, Archbishop Edward T. O'Meara authorized the diocesan personnel board to prepare plans to deal with the anticipated loss of fifteen percent of his 146 priests by the year 1987. Father David Coats, director of personnel, announced a plan calling for parish clusters served by joint staffs of priests, the regional assignment of priests, and the appointment of pastoral ministers who are not priests to some of the clustered parishes. In the diocese of Great Falls-Billings, Montana, Bishop Thomas Murphy appointed a task force to deal with the anticipated shortage of priests in that area. Working with Father Thomas Sweetser, S.J., of the Parish Evaluation Project, the group, composed of priests, religious, and laity, confronted the prediction of a rising Catholic population and a loss of more than half of the present 98 priests by the year 2000. They developed proposals for groupings of parishes under larger faith communities, the inclusion of laity in more ministry and administration, and other programs similar to those being discussed in other parts of the country. There was extensive lay involvement in the eighteen months of the task force's work. The Rev. David Dwyer, chairman, said that the process was giving the laity their "rightful position in the church."

Similar experiments are going on, among other places, in Minnesota, Wisconsin, and Texas. One can safely predict that they will multiply rapidly over the next five years. What is important about these developments is that they are sanctioned by the official Church, they are rooted in the collegial process, and they represent behavioral changes, most of which can be put immediately into effect in terms of the revised code of canon law. Still, these projects tell only part of the story of Catholicism's gearing up for the future in America. In many areas these planned changes have already occurred. This behavioral-level change, far better than attitude scales, tells us what future American Catholicism will be like. In almost every section of the country religious men and women, in large numbers, have moved into aspects of pastoral ministry in parishes, hospitals, and schools. Nonpriests, frequently nuns, have been designated pastors as, for example, Sister Jouvann at St. James Parish in Dawson, Minnesota. Such examples could be multiplied readily throughout the country. The American Church is not falling apart as much as it is pulling itself effectively together for the future which, in many ways, has already arrived. Something is already being done—and will not be undone—about the problems of ministerial personnel for the next century.

Pressures for change also come from outside America. Major transformation will obviously take place because of the shift of the Church's center of gravity to the Third World, particularly Africa. The ghosts of old battles will fade as these newer churches assert themselves and their own national heritages, enriching the overall life of the Church and accenting its universality as they do so. Instead of drawing all things to Rome, Rome will increasingly be drawn out to embrace the wealth of diversity in the human family it serves. Issues such as celibacy will not be debated away; they will rather become less important and will be resolved in the context of a Church no longer strongly identified with the bitter struggles of Western Europe in the Middle Ages.

The American Church will not be surprised at such changes. It already feels them in its bones and has in place the collegial machinery to negotiate them in an orderly manner under the leadership of bishops and priests who, in classic American fashion, pragmatically perceive the ecclesiastical evolution that is under way. The solutions will not come from the golden age of clericalism, from, for example, the cadres of married deacons who have been ordained over the past fifteen years. Married deacons represent a past, temporary accommodation with a clerically dominated Church. As such, they are anachronistic and fit marginally, if at all, into the future. They will be remembered as a significant transitional presence which helped condition the Church for its greater lay character.

Catholicism's face and customs will also be altered by the steady rise of a new immigrant Church. Just as the country is feeling the impact of the expanding Hispanic culture in the Southwest and Southeast, so the Church finds itself markedly affected by the increasing numbers of Latin Catholics. They bring new attitudes and traditions to worship, Church support, and vocations. The incorporation of the energies and customs of these Latin

Catholics will be a major factor in the remaking of American Catholicism over the next twenty years.

The now and future Church is already here, feeling its way toward tomorrow by making practical changes today. These represent, under powerful eucharistic symbols, a death to sweet memories and traditions that looked as if they would last forever. This transition, energized by new immigrant peoples, is the ordinary face of the religious experience spoken of by Joseph Campbell. American Catholics are involved in letting go of something they once treasured in order to be able to take it up again with renewed appreciation. We are being called out of bondage to see the world and each other more clearly in the space age.

The Shape of Things to Come

IN THE LIGHT of the dynamics that have come to govern the activity of the American Church, as well as the behavioral changes that have already taken place, the following predictions can be made about the next generation of Catholic life.

1. The dominant mode of existence has passed definitely from confrontation to negotiation. The disciplinary issues of the coming years will not be effectively settled by episcopal or papal *fiat* because that technique simply does not work any more. More importantly, neither people, theologians, nor bishops are in a mood for divisive argument. Despite deep convictions—and the healthy tension that is inevitable when varying viewpoints clash—Catholics do not wish to fight with each other or with their leaders any more. Collegiality and its varied forums for discussion will prevail if only because everything else will fail. The Church's administrators are by now battle-scarred enough to understand that their flocks cannot be whipped into orderly military phalanxes

of obedient believers in the postimmigrant phase of American Catholicism. The bishops appreciate the fact that, drawn out and laborious as the method may be, they can only speak to their people if they listen to them first. The American Church has passed, as a healthy couple may in a good marriage, beyond the stage of needing to prove that someone is right and someone is wrong in every discussion. The present era insofar as it succeeds will be one of collaboration and dialogue.

The Bernardin era will make progress because its style is not adversarial; it does not seek confrontation but rather invites dissenters to join their opinions to the process of discussion. The notion that a right wing of the American Church will group itself around New York's Archbishop John O'Connor as a balancing force makes for good journalism but it is unrealistic. Archbishop O'Connor's temperament and style are not those of a dissenter but those of a strong supporter of the modern, orthodox center led by men like Bernardin. While O'Connor may seem a throwback to the tough, confident archbishops of generations past, he needs and seeks cooperation with approval from the leadership he respects. Such dissent as he offers will, therefore, invigorate the collegial process.

Indeed, only the hardiest and the most committed will be willing to stick to the process which, nonetheless, will prevail. The main problem for the future is not guaranteeing this style of progressive discussion but of encouraging educated Catholics, clerical, religious, and lay, to take part in it. The vitality of the American Church depends far more on educating its people to their responsibilities for continuing participation in formal Church matters than in attempting to control the nature or outcome of that participation. As of the mid-eighties there are many thousands of well-educated Catholics willing to bear the burdens of responsibility for the work of the Church. Involving them more than perfunctorily—taking them seriously as Christians—in the dialogues on the pressing issues of our time to which the bishops have committed themselves will guarantee a healthy and constructive pastoral presence in the country.

2. If dialogue will be the preferred and only workable means to further the preaching of the gospel and the resolution of administrative issues within the Church, the effective involvement of large numbers of lay people in Church life will be perceived as the bishops' major responsibility. This will be far more significant than doomed efforts to restore the vocational supply of priests and religious to the dizzying heights that were achieved by immigrant Catholicism. The bishops are highly intelligent and wonderfully pragmatic. They feel keenly the obligation to keep the Church as an institution alive and functioning. Coming finally to an understanding that times truly have changed, they will abandon the tactics of vocational recruitment that are now as outdated and ineffective as the regal *pronunciamentos* of fifty years ago. They will accept the fact that ministry, rather than minor seminarians, is the overriding concern of a Church that is determined to preach the gospel of Jesus in the next century. As they have given themselves to the process of collegiality among themselves, so they will extend it, first out of necessity and later out of insight, to the sincere inclusion of the laity in carrying out the pastoral administration of the Church.

Up until now, many bishops, by clerical habits of mind difficult for even the most enlightened among them to overcome, have coped with the newly proclaimed rights and roles of the laity instead of wholeheartedly embracing them or the theology that is their foundation. Future dialogue on great issues—and on the homely details of everyday pastoral practice—will concern itself with in-corporating laymen, and especially laywomen, without qualification or conditions into responsible partnership with the bishops. Much of the groundwork for this has already been done, some true conversion of heart has taken place among the bishops that has cleansed them of the residual paternalism handed down to them from the high culture of clericalism, but the test of actually taking the laity seriously—of operationally understanding that the people are indeed the Church—looms now before them. That is the complicated problem whose successful resolution will determine the character of American Ca-tholicism in the next century.

3. Women constitute the most important group in the American Church. They are yet to be accepted as full-fledged citizens of the Kingdom, even though it is hardly an exaggeration to claim that the strength and achieve-ments of American Catholicism are due largely to them. The early eighties witnessed what will one day be identi-fied as the incredible and unnecessary estrangement of many of these women from the Church for reasons that were theologically indefensible, pastorally wasteful, and humanly tragic. Pope John Paul II has come dangerously close to expressing attitudes toward women that are con-descending, Old World, and classically clerical. He does not seem to appreciate that the movement of women toward practical equality transcends the Catholic Church and that as one of the major dynamics of twenti-eth-century history, it constitutes a clear sign of the times that can be misread or ignored only at one's own peril. The women's movement within the Catholic Church is not some collection of angry feminists who, like Garibaldi's soldiers, must be defeated before they seize the Vatican State. The continuing vigor of the Church is intimately related to a new consciousness of

women as essential to its own self-understanding and to carrying out its mission in the world.

Practically speaking, then, the tentative maneuvering between church officials and the women who demand active recognition of their equality must be abandoned and replaced by hard, sensible, open negotiations based on theologically sound principles and a less defensive posture. Anybody who underestimates the intelligence, maturity, and determination of the Church's women, particularly its religious women, makes a mistake of enormous proportions. Mishandling or postponing the frank and open resolution of this issue will one day be judged a tactical error at the end of the century as grave as that made at its beginning through the repression of progressive scholarship and seminary education. Make no misjudgment: working out the conflict over an expanding role for women within it is the main business and moral obligation of the American Church in the next decade. It is not so much that they must immediately be granted priestly ordination (that will come in the next century) but that they must be given a respectful hearing that acknowledges the Church's debt to them in the past and desperate need for them in the future. If this can be managed well, a great many other questions, including many of those concerned with human sexuality, marriage, and the family, will also be successfully resolved. Failing to incorporate women more responsibly in the Church will also keep in place that very dynamic that for so long has made the full exploration of these issues so difficult and divisive.

What can one predict? Increased and more sincerely open dialogue with the American bishops who must, at the same time, publicly defend the statements of the Pope and the tradition of the Church in keeping women in what can only be described as second-class citizenship. Progress will be more rapid as the failure to find new sources of old-style vocations becomes more obvious. The inability to summon up the old days of the immigrant Church will gradually be understood not as evidence of secularity, selfishness, or a lack of faith in young people, but as proof that a new order of living has, in fact, evolved during the twentieth century, that it has profoundly affected the sociological reality of the Church, and that it cannot be undone. The bishops will accommodate eventually, although there will be considerable and unnecessary suffering in the interlude before dawn. A full accommodation waits on the next papal election.

4. A new papal election will also be necessary for the follow-through advances that are essential to the ecumenical movement. While there has been extraordinary progress, for example, in resolving theological differences between Catholics and Episcopalians as well as Catholics and Lutherans, Pope John Paul II, while authoring potent symbolic gestures of good will, such as praying with the Archbishop of Canterbury and preaching in Rome's Lutheran Church, has hesitated to take the further, essential steps that would lead to Christian reunion. His reluctance to go beyond his generous gestures of brotherhood has caused concern among non-Catholic Christian leaders who, while grateful for his support, understand that these are not enough to resolve divisions in Christendom. John Paul, wary of anything that may further obscure the identity of the Roman Church, has gone as far as he can or will go in exercising leadership in this cause.

Progress will nonetheless continue between the churches in much the same way that it does within them. The behavioral changes—the actions people are willing to take, based on deepened understandings of each other's viewpoints and a meeting of minds on theological points—will ultimately determine the nature and rate of ecumenical progress in the next century. Pope John Paul II's studied approach to reunion reveals him as a man who lives in the old and the new world at the same time. He cannot, however, prevent educated Christians from coming to conclusions for which they will not feel the need for his approval. Seeing that theologians agree on the teachings of various Christian churches, men and women will reach ecumenical arrangements about prayer, worship, and the sacraments, including inter-communion, that will put them in front of the official church and subtly but profoundly change the self-aware-ness of the Christian believing community.

The essential changes of the coming decade will not follow from agreements or documents signed and sealed by church officials but from the already well-established attitudes and behavior of the believing community. As illustrated in the parable of the two sons, one of whom promised to do what his father wished but did not, while the other refused and then carried out his father's wishes, what people actually *do* tells us far more than what they say they will do. The best predictions about tomorrow are based on what people are doing today. These are the only reliable megatrends.

A close look at the behavior of the Catholic commu-nity might startle many ecclesiastical leaders who have no real idea of the far-advanced transformation of Amer-ican Catholic consciousness. It is obvious that on levels of sexual relationships, Catholics have made decisive state-ments they are not likely to change. Using their own freedom of conscience and taking their moral and famil-ial obligations seriously, they choose not to believe that contraception is intrinsically evil. They have remarkably changed attitudes—and are willing to act differently—

about divorce and remarriage. There is evidence, in fact, that while they accept the ideal of indissolubility, they realize that the Church, in granting annulments compassionately over the last several years, has also changed its practice in regard to marriage. Catholics who have been granted annulments do not necessarily think that they were not truly married to their original spouses. They accept a procedure that presently allows remarriage by declaring that no previous marriage existed. To many believers this is a harmful distortion of reality that would be better served if the Church came to more realistic terms with the fact of divorce. The enormous changes of attitude that have taken place over the last generation will push this issue to the forefront within the next ten years. While this will generate great tension within the official Church, the impulse to close the gap in its thinking about marriage and divorce possesses the compelling logic of deeply felt human experience. A successful managing of this question will demand a pastoral deftness of a high order. It cannot be avoided because it affects the entire community of the faithful.

The country's bishops might also be surprised to learn how, even within the most devout Catholic families, compromises are being struck every day on questions that people would never previously have addressed on their own. Today, however, when men and women encounter unreasonable or, sadly enough at times, incompetent and theologically retrograde clergy, they often take matters into their own hands and resolve difficult issues with peaceful consciences. Here too marriage is the focus of concern. Good Catholics are willing to accept second marriages, marriages that end up being performed in non-Catholic settings or through a "pastoral" understanding with a cooperative priest. They accept these largely because on the experiential level they have witnessed too much heartbreak and too much unhappiness generated by strict adherence to Church requirements which they have come to perceive as inconsistent, historically conditioned, and having been administered too often by men with only the most remote conception of what marriage and family life actually demand of human beings.

Catholics want to cooperate with the Church. They want the blessing, the sacramental reinforcement, the communal support that a parish offers in a way that no other social entity can. They will not, however, destroy their children's chances for happiness—or at least for relative contentment—by insisting on the kind of adherence to clerical wishes that was common in the great days of the immigrant Church. As yet there is little reliable information on the extent to which Catholics are willing to live in good faith—and in communion with the Church—with exceptions to demands of canon law. Perhaps the most powerful—and characteristically American—impulse beneath these changes is the desire for relationships that are real rather than hypocritical or ecclesiastical fictions.

One photograph, printed on the front pages of the world's newspapers last winter, richly symbolized both the elements of the immigrant Church experience and the transformations that have taken place in recent years. It showed Princess Caroline of Monaco, her second husband at her side, her father, Prince Rainier III, smiling behind her, as she responded to the cheering citizens of Monaco below the palace window. One must remember that the princess is the granddaughter of an Irish-American contractor from Philadelphia on the one hand and an heiress to a "Let's Pretend" vestige of European monarchy on the other, two constituent elements of the high culture of the immigrant Church. Her mother, the late Princess Grace, was married in a lavish cathedral ceremony in Monte Carlo in 1956, with ecclesiastics of various ranks smiling proudly in the background. Princess Grace lived a life of extraordinary public Catholicity, a symbol, in many ways, of the best of the immigrant phase of the American Church. That a daughter of hers would be married before her first marriage had been officially annulled would have been for her unthinkable, as, indeed, any comparable experience would have been for thousands of Catholic families whose roots were in the obedient immigrant Church. But, in fact, with Prince Rainier's apparent approval and support, that is exactly what took place. The event reflects vividly the changed perceptions of the generation of once rigidly orthodox Catholics of Princess Grace's generation. They have seen too much sadness, as has been noted, to drive their children away from them because the mills of the official Church grind slowly. They feel no less Catholic for accepting responsibility for decisions which would have been unimaginable in the Catholic community a generation ago. This reality, howsoever one may judge it, cannot be denied. The leaders of the American Church might well meditate on that photograph, so telling in so many ways, about the psychological reality of contemporary American Catholicism.

This reality is intimately related to Catholic attitudes toward the clergy. These are still marked by deference and respect, but even the most street-smart of American bishops might be amazed to learn the true feelings of many Catholics for their priests. The clergy of the country are getting older and many are getting weary. They retire with regularity, die according to the insurance tables just like everyone else; they are a valiant but vanishing generation. Bishops in some places have made uncomfortable compromises in their attempts to cover their pastoral obligations with men of diminished energy and enthusiasm and, at times, questionable ability. The ranks grow thinner every year, and while most Catholics appreciate the earnestness of their clergy, they are well prepared for radical changes to replace them when it is necessary. This is already demonstrated behaviorally in the experiments and planning for priestless parishes in many parts of the country. What ecclesiastical leaders may not know is with what ease and confidence mature believers would accept the ordination of their own members to serve as celebrants of the Eucharistic mystery. Adult Catholics are well prepared to see themselves as the source for the vocations of the future, and their common-sense theological feeling for the situation is remarkably close to that espoused by some of the Church's most orthodox and penetrating thinkers.

Will the bishops begin to ordain men—and later, women—from the Christian community to preside over the Eucharist and carry out other aspects of the sacramental ministry? Many episcopal leaders are prepared to do exactly that and, indeed, one can anticipate that this is exactly what will happen before this century ends. The reasons will be partly theological, partly because some leaders have extraordinary vision, but mostly because the future of the Church as an effective institution will come to depend on just such moves.

By the 1990s one may anticipate that psychosocial realities will favor once again a search for transcendence through lives of service rather than strategies of self-improvement. The latter remain dominant in the mideighties, although there are signs of progressive dissatisfaction with lives in which men and women focus so strongly on themselves and their own interests. People are growing tired of the psychological consumerism that allows numerous choices and makes few demands on them; they are weary of not growing up on time, of being psychologically disabled by the availability of gratifications for themselves, of life-style, in other words, as a substitute for life. There will be a rediscovery of some of the staples of a truly human existence: the value of delaying rather than insisting on immediate gratification; the role of sacrifice in the stabilization of relationships; the profound need to live for something greater than the self in order to achieve a spiritual sense; the role of healthy authority in basic human communities. Men and women will be ready for a call to service in the ministerial work of the Church. Church officials should realize that there will be plenty of laborers to help with the harvest, that the ache for spiritual experience will be so great that the Church should not be surprised by it or unprepared to respond to it.

The American bishops of the mideighties, as the fine harvest of the latter days of the immigrant Church, realize that, as previously noted, their pool of replacements is dangerously low and that serious questions have been raised about the quality of some of those who now seek to enter seminaries. Their choice is becoming stark and simple. They can begin to ordain an inferior grade of clergy in order to fill the empty places in the priesthood. They would do this, however, at the risk of weakening the ranks of the priesthood and, in the course of time, of the episcopate as well. Their commitment, however, is to institutional continuity, something that cannot be achieved if both the numbers and quality of the priesthood diminish. The visible, structured Church that struggles to contain and express the mystery of Christ's Church can only survive sociologically if it maintains a high level of episcopal leadership. Other Church bodies that have allowed their clergy to weaken have become progressively more amorphous and uncertain of themselves. That is the possibility for the American Catholic Church in the next century—a diffuse, rambling organization that gambled away its future by failing to prepare for it practically and adequately.

The present generation of American bishops is too shrewd to allow this to happen. We can anticipate, then, that by 1990 innovative recruitment of priests from among adult Catholics will replace the rusted machinery of vocational development left over from the bustling, obsessive era of immigrant Church life. It is not, as a matter of fact, a radically new idea but one that dates from the earliest days of the Church. The American Church will change—and give good reasons for it—and thereby dispose itself to continuing change in the next century. At the same time, one can happily anticipate that it will preach the gospel of Jesus more clearly and that it will restore many of the customs and practices, such as opportunities for the Latin mass and the treasures of Gregorian chant that are presently stored in its vast attic. These will be incidental, however, for a Church which, much to the surprise of Pope John Paul II, is remarkably energetic, inventive, and faithful to its mission.

The Myth of Servanthood

THERE EXISTS a myth with which the concerned Catholics of the day can well identify. Through it bishops, priests, religious, and lay people can perceive their essential oneness with each other. It is the powerful biblical myth of servanthood. Through it the central psychological experience for Catholics will be not the obligation to keep rules, as it was in the immigrant Church, but to follow a call to service. This myth can support the Church as it embarks on a generation of transformation.

How, in fact, does the notion of servanthood meet the requirements of being an adequate myth for our times? According to Joseph Campbell, the first function of a living mythology, "the properly religious function," is "to awaken and maintain in the individual an experience of awe, humility, and respect, in recognition of that ultimate mystery, transcending names and forms. . . ." There is something ineffable, something beyond words, in the sense of the transcendent mystery into which we are incorporated by an effective mythology. So it is with the notion of servanthood whose implications cannot be quite fully defined because it breaks us free of time and place to involve us in a sense of continuity and religious expectation that leads us always beyond ourselves.

The second function of mythology, according to Campbell, "is to render a cosmology, an image of the universe that matches our deepest spiritual understanding." The notion of servanthood collapses the distinctions made about the wide universe itself. The unity of our experience gives us a sense that there is no broad line drawn across creation on one side of which things can be labeled secular and on the other side of which things can be labeled sacred. In the Lord there is neither Jew nor Greek, neither slave nor freeman. This myth of servanthood implies a return to a feeling for our God-given unity and for the unity of God's creation; it offers a new map in which we can find our way as whole rather than divided persons, in which we realize better our oneness with each other.

The third function of a living myth is "the validation and maintenance of an established order." The myth of servanthood is not linked to preconceived notions but to the bedrock of ongoing human experience and need, the sense of redemption not worked out beforehand but minute by minute as we steadily bring ourselves more fully to life. It is the theme for a time in which people are aware of the demands of their own consciences and of their own responsibility for fashioning the moral shape of their lives. There is something terrifying about it, this openness to the grace of service in an unpredictable world. What other image could better describe believers who prove their faith by giving themselves away to others in ministry in a renewing Church?

The fourth function of a living mythology is, according to Campbell, "the centering and harmonization of the individual." An effective myth must reinforce our sense of individual responsibility as well as our feeling for being members of a people together. Servanthood does not ask us to subject ourselves to the control of some higher authority; it invites us to commit ourselves with as much awareness as possible to the design of our own religious destiny. Servanthood is an invitation to take our existence seriously and not to let someone else supervise it or control it too closely. We have witnessed the death of that blind obedience that matched the model of monarchy. It is an achievement of Christian development that we return now to the state of being servants who are not slaves but persons who realize fully the dignity of their calling and of their obedience to the needs of mankind. Servanthood is a voluntary state; its richness flows from the freedom with which people join themselves to it. The meaning of servanthood lies in the power of love that is its only energy as well as the only sign of the Spirit that is completely trustworthy.

This myth is already inhabited by believers who understand the enormous needs of the world and who search for a recognition of their own religious impulse to serve it with whatever gifts they have. Ministry is a reliable myth for the religious experience of Catholics in the twenty-first century, for it says that faith can never be just a private affair or a personal comfort. Our future does not lie in outmoded theologies but in understanding the public nature of the service expected of the people who are ministers by baptism. It is not a question of *whether* believers are called but of *how* they are called to minister. Servanthood is rich in choice: some are called for a lifetime, some for a year, some for part of every one of their years. The servants bring the gifts they have and risk them instead of burying them in the ground. There is nothing new in this myth, but there is everything fresh and energizing for those who understand that being a Catholic means taking on the form of a servant rather than of a master. The most exciting religious awareness of this era centers on ministry as the vocation shared by all believers by virtue of their baptism.

What can be done in a practical manner about this? We need, of course, an amplified understanding of the Christian vocation to service. That arises from a return to vocation as a public call to one of a variety of ministries. We do not look now for a return to an old-fashioned vocational supply, of seminaries and novitiates refitted like a mothball fleet refurbished for war. The vocations are present throughout the Church in the lay people who have already proved their willingness to take up their share of ministry in collaboration with priests and religious. They do this now freely rather than from obsessive-compulsive pressures.

The ministries of the now and future Church are as varied as its people are, and they are, by and large, already engaged in them. The challenge is not to enroll old-style and tender-aged vocational prospects but to recognize the vocations of service already being lived out all around us. We need to validate these vocations through a public symbolic recognition and continued call of these people to ministry. The limits of the Church's pastoral imagination are the only limits to its ability to respond operationally to the contemporary consciousness of the ministry that is the function of the whole Church. So, on the practical level, we need a formal call issued by the American bishops and, in each diocese, a plan to recognize and incorporate these ministries into the active pastoral life of the Church. Nothing less than this will cure what exaggerated clericalism has done to the Church.

Obviously, women are to be taken far more seriously

as full partners in the ministry of the Church. They cannot merely be pacified and kept somehow at bay. The women of the American Church have been largely responsible for its achievements. These women have a new sense of themselves and their potential for reviewing the ministerial vocation of the whole Church. They will not be put off by assertions by male ecclesiastics, no matter how highly placed, that their time has not come or that enormous theological difficulties exist around the subject of women priests. These women want to work through these difficulties rather than be put off by them; even though many of them may not wish to become priests, all of them want to take on mature ministerial responsibilities—and receive the recognition due them—in the pastoral work of the Church.

A further practical step centers on the support of adult and continuing education programs throughout each diocese. The frameworks that already exist provide the setting for expanded ministerial preparation and pastoral development. What remains of the seminary system, for example, provides the facilities to prepare together all the people who are capable of exercising a share in contemporary ministry. The effort to recreate seminaries as solely for clerics is bound to fail. Clerics isolated in seminaries are as frustrated as the ministering persons with whom they will eventually work if they are prepared on a two-track or split-level system. Seminaries, which have yet to be as radically renewed as they might have been had Driscoll succeeded at Dunwoodie, provide the appropriate symbolic setting for preparing people to take up their ministerial responsibilities. A consciousness that all Christians are called publicly to tithe of their lives and talents in ministry makes seminaries the symbols of a new and vigorous age rather than relics of one gone by.

Many other practical steps can be taken right now at the parish level to convey a sense of the Church's commitment to servanthood, not as the exalted life of perfection reserved for a few, but as the basic condition of Christian life offered to all imperfect believers. Servanthood is a myth strong and deep enough to sustain a believing people in a new age. One takes courage from the hint of an invitation to all of us who are simultaneously faulted and gifted in Christ's commission of Peter. It is the very kind of thing men and women heard at the beginning of this century and, save for repression, might have preached much earlier. It is an aspect of the overall myth of servanthood, the ministry shared by the less than perfect. "You do not understand spiritual things," Christ says to Peter, "I will make you head of my Church." The vocation to ministry is issued to all of us who do not quite understand spiritual things either. That is the saving irony of profoundly religious experience. It is the promise of the power of the postimmigrant Church in the interstellar age.

INDEX

EUGENE KENNEDY, author of many books, twice the recipient of the Thomas More Medal for contributions to Catholic literature, has also received the Carl Sandburg Award for both nonfiction and fiction, as well as the award of the Society of Midwest Authors and the Chicago Foundation of Literature. He is a professor of psychology at Loyola University of Chicago.